SISTER/ STRANGER:

Lesbians Loving Across the Lines

Edited by
Jan Hardy

Sidewalk Revolution Press

P.O. Box 9062 Pittsburgh PA 15224

Grateful acknowledgement is made for permission to use the following previously published material:

"Navigating by Stars" by Donna Allegra first appeared in *Common Lives/Lesbian Lives*, Spring 1992.

"Think Twice Before You Call Me Courageous Again" by Elizabeth Clare first appeared in *Sinister Wisdom*, Summer/Fall 1988.

"If" and "Impatient Womanifesto" by Amy Edgington first appeared in *Common Lives/Lesbian Lives*, Fall 1987.

"Personality or Politics?" by Nett Hart first appeared in *Feminist Bookstore News*, Sept./Oct. 1991 and in *Woman of Power*, Winter/Spring 1992.

"Disability and Intimacy" by Sandra Lambert first appeared in *Common Lives/Lesbian Lives*, Spring 1988.

"A poem for the white middle class lesbian who insists I am just like her" by Janet Mason first appeared in *Sojourner*, February 1991.

"That Great Divide" by Pam Mitchell first appeared in *Bridges: A Journal for Jewish Feminists and Our Friends*, Fall 1991.

"Who Will Lead?" by Cristina Salat first appeared in *Writing For Our Lives Literary Journal*, Spring/Summer 1992.

"The Same Moon" by Ruth L. Schwartz first appeared in *Outlook*, May 1991.

"Thin Friends' Pantoum" by Susan Stinson first appeared in *Common Lives/Lesbian Lives*, Spring 1987.

"To a Lover/Twenty Years Younger" by Lois Van Houten first appeared in *All Those Bells* (NJ: Stone Country Press, 1981); "Giving Quarter" by Lois Van Houten first appeared in *The Woman Wedged in the Window* (NJ: Ahnoi Press, 1979).

"The Measurements" by Colleen M. Webster first appeared in *World of Poetry* (Sacramento, CA), 1991.

"ability and will" by zana first appeared in *Maize: A Lesbian Country Magazine*, Spring 1988, and in *Hikane: The Capable Womon*, Autumn 1989.
ISBN: 0961740639

Acknowledgements

Many people provided support and random acts of kindness, without which *Sister/Stranger* would still be a concept and not a book. First, my love and thanks always to Pat Amplas, who believed in me from the start, listened to all my worries, pushed gently when I needed it, lived with me through it all, and still loves me! Jean Sirius, typesetter and designer extraordinaire, also appeared as editor, proofreader, spiritual guide and e-mail buddy. Many thanks to Sharon Plataz for her beautiful cover design, and to Sally Graham for her assistance. Cathy Palmisano helped tremendously with proofreading. The Gertrude Stein Memorial Bookshop wimmin graciously granted me time away from meetings and work shifts to complete this book; may their coffers increase (ching ching!). My friends in the Pittsburgh wimmin's community inquired kindly and often about *Sister/Stranger*'s progress (or lack thereof), and encouraged me with their enthusiasm. Last but not least, I owe a debt of gratitude to each of the contributors for their words, their willingness to work out details, and their bravery in writing, and loving, across the lines.

Table of Contents

for Pat—
(wishing I could find the words)
and for all the lesbians who love across the lines

Introduction

by Jan Hardy

Editing this anthology has been a joy, a privilege, and an absolute terror. The subject, lesbians loving across differences of race, class, ethnic and religious backgrounds, age, size, and ability, was enormous. Many collections could be gathered and published without doing it justice. Many books which focus on the differences and identities among women, lesbian or not, have already been published by feminist presses: *Nice Jewish Girls: A Lesbian Anthology, With the Power of Each Breath: A Disabled Women's Anthology, Look Me In the Eye: Old Women, Aging, and Ageism*, and *This Bridge Called My Back: Writings by Radical Women of Color*, to name just a few. Journals like *Lesbian Ethics, Fireweed, Sinister Wisdom*, and *Bridges* have published special issues on women and class. This is a very partial listing, and, thankfully, many more titles detailing the variety of lesbian lives continue to be published.[1]

All of these titles contain pieces about lesbians loving (or arguing) across differences, as well as accounts of lesbians focussing on their own needs and strengths, their own identities and groups. As a separatist, I'm totally supportive of any group building strength from within, rather than joining in coalitions, and I know that struggling across differences may not always be what's needed.

So why did I feel this book was necessary? Part of the answer lies in my coming-out story, which probably mirrors the stories of many lesbians like me who are white, mid-30's, able-bodied, gentile, middle-class. For me, coming out in the mid-1970's was like stepping into a warm sauna filled with loving, accepting women. Always tense and on my guard, I could finally relax and let down my defenses; always a loner, I suddenly had a community of friends, allies, lovers, a refuge from sexism and homophobia. The words I remember hearing most often during those years were "support" and "visibility." What a high

---

[1]For a more complete listing, please see "Suggestions for Further Reading" on p. 174.

it was to have both, after years of confusion and isolation.

Like Joanna Kadi, "I believed the rhetoric that 'Sisterhood is beautiful.' It's a tad embarrassing to admit now, but I honestly expected lesbian lovers would be equals because of our femaleness." ("Love, Space Aliens, and Politics," p. 97) For a while, I even believed that "our" community didn't have to deal with racism, ableism, classism, ageism, fat-phobia, or anti-Semitism, since all oppression stemmed from the sexism at the root of patriarchy. Once we "got rid of" sexism, the other forms of oppression would somehow disappear. I remember arguing with an African-American woman that her first allegiance should be with the feminist movement, not the civil rights movement, and I brushed her off with a sense of superiority when she rightly refused to make that choice.

But when the fog lifted and I began to hear what other women were saying, I realized that the comfort, support and visibility many lesbians enjoyed in "our" community wasn't often extended to lesbians who are of color, who are poor or working-class, fat, disabled, old, Jewish. And though lesbian-feminist agendas of the 1990's are usually careful to include lists of "isms" in our battles against bigotry, these words too rarely translate into action.

Building a personal friendship sounds like it should be easier than building a movement; however, another inspiration for this book came from my lover's comment that most lesbians choose friends who are "just like us" in terms of class, age, race, religion, and ethnicity. The more I thought about this, the more shocked I was, for in spite of the few exceptions I could point to, most of my friends *were* "just like me." "It's natural," my lover said, "we just feel more comfortable with people who share our experiences." But was it always necessary to be that comfortable, to have an exact reflection of myself with whom I could share my time? Why was difference so often uncomfortable?

Because I could make mistakes, I realized. Because I could very easily, especially in a casual setting, let something slip and put my foot in my mouth. And I'd rather talk a good line and look good than make messy mistakes.

This revelation still comes back to me, still haunts me as I go about my days and nights and interactions in the lesbian community. Like any lesbian feminist revelation, it takes a lifetime of hard work to make an inch of progress. But I carry it with me, not to induce guilt, but to push me to reach more often across the lines.

Focussing on lover and friend relationships was one way to narrow down the material for this book, and my own relationship was the third inspiration for *Sister/Stranger*. As I type this, a lesbian we've hired as a babysitter keeps my lover's six-year-old granddaughter occupied in the living room down the hall. I love a woman twelve years older than me, who comes from a mostly lower-class childhood, who escaped her marriage to survive as a single mother of four, who suffers chronic back pain from a work-related injury. I was raised, as I mentioned, mostly middle-class in a stable, secure environment; I have a college education, no dependents, no disabilities. Our differences have been tough teachers, at times subtle and confusing, at other times glaring and scary. These few sentences don't do justice to my lover and what she survived, to our love or to her patience. I had hoped to write a piece for this anthology, but found the work of editing too involving (and the story of my lover and me too overwhelming!). Although our story may not appear on these pages, I offer the book itself, as tribute and thanks.

Which brings me to the necessary apologia. The absolute terror I referred to earlier was this: given the immensity of the subject of lesbians loving across differences, and given the physical limitations of publishing, some shortcomings were inevitable. I miss the voices of more old lesbians, and the younger women who love them, to give just one example.

As it is, this book includes work by 35 lesbians from all over the U.S., as well as from Canada, the U.K. and Australia. The contributors are women of color and white women, Jewish and gentile, working-class, poor and middle-class; they are thin and fat, able-bodied and disabled, and their ages range from early 20's to early 70's. They tell of their fears, angers, arguments, and the everyday miracles of humor and understanding. And of course, being lesbians, they tell of the erotic passion and loving affection that can bloom between women, whatever our differences.

I suppose that in gathering these stories, poems, and essays, I was looking for answers, for myself and for lesbians everywhere who are beginning to feel the limitations of staying within our comfortable boundaries. How do we build a truly multicultural movement? How do we reach across differences, gain understanding, and create access? Over and over, in many different words and images, the contributors replied: ask questions, listen carefully, communicate, and act on what you learn. The words might be hard to find—after all, it's easier to assume, assimilate, be silent, be "polite," overlook. The answers, whether spoken in anger or love, may be hard to hear—but we need to keep listening. And above all, lesbians who have some privileges need to stop expecting other lesbians to do all the work, including the work of what we used to call consciousness-raising. Jodi, in "Loving In Spite of Mistakes," puts it this way:

> "What do I ask of others, on *my* issues? Interest, growing levels of awareness, an openness of spirit. I want them to read and think about our literature. I want them to educate each other, speak up in public places, feel and act as if it matters, and not think they're doing me a favor...
> I want to know that everything we do comes out of love instead of guilt." (p. 24)

Or, as Donna Allegra's character says to her newfound lover in "Navigating by Stars," "I want for you to see where I live and know who I am... and I wonder who you are." (p. 164)

We know by now that it's not easy, and it doesn't come automatically as we enter the lesbian community; what we do know, more than ever, is just how vital our connections are to the life of this movement. And whether we reach toward a political alliance, friendship, romance, or all three at once, that spark of connection across the lines can enrich our lives in ways we are just beginning to explore.

SISTER/ STRANGER:

Lesbians Loving Across the Lines

Edited by
Jan Hardy

Gwendolyn Bikis

Blue Sky

This story is for Paulette.

"Sunday Brunch" was what our college's foodservice staff called it; what they meant was Your Last Chance to Eat Before Supper. "Dinner," the Carolinians among us called it. What it was, was a sweet or greasy breakfast arrayed alongside a wide variety of dinner leftovers. Tastee-Do donuts and mushy eggs, lifeless vegetables and carefully disguised meats. Peanut butter for the fainthearted.

We'd gone through the food line, gotten our milks and coffees, and chosen this sunny corner table together. At this table, almost every Sunday, the four of us shared at least one long meal, smoking, drinking weak coffee, and talking the afternoon away. The Four of Us were Paul and Rodney, me, and Tammy. Four Reduced to Three, in fact, because none of us this morning had any idea where Tammy was. Nor had we last night, when the three of us had gotten so high and silly that we'd all awakened with the munchies. Even so, the food was a deterrent.

"Damn," sighed Rodney, "Mama didn't need to send me to no fat farm this summer. She could've just sent me here. You can not no way tell me that *dis* is not Alpo meat." He dropped his fork, sneered weakly, and sat back in his chair.

"Damn," I took up the chorus, "These grits are the grayest I've seen this side of the bus station."

It was a ritual, begun by Tammy last spring.

Paul arrived and unloaded his tray (three plates, three glasses, two cups and a bowl), then sat and dipped into his yogurt. "A little runny," he remarked, and slurped. "And definitely thin." He dipped his spoon in again. "Not bad, though, for yogurt soup."

Paul would eat most anything, Tammy had observed more than once to me.

I leaned back, crossing my legs away from the table. Rodney lit a cigarette. I reached for my chocolate milk, glancing at the empty chair between me and Rodney. We were all three waiting for Tammy.

I was draining my second glass of chocolate milk, with my eye tipped toward the door, when Tammy walked in, with less swing than usual in her walk. She paused to drop her keys in her dress pocket, and I saw, while her eyes passed over the lunchroom, how droopy were her cheeks and eyelids. I watched her when she turned to get her tray. I waited while she filled her plate and glasses and collected her silverware.

As usual, I watched the inside of her arms, the flex and bulge of her biceps, as she lowered her tray to the table. But why were her elbows so ashy—I glanced away from the gray and smudgy skin—and why was her hair "all ragged ed-ged," as she herself would call it? I knew Tammy's morning ablutions too well—her washing and brushings, combings and anointings—to not suspect that something was wrong.

She sat, looked slowly at her food. Her lips twitched. "Damn," she shook her head. "This corn bread look about as tasty as an old dry sponge to me." She tossed the cornbread against the side of her tray, jerked back her chair, and got up to get "some damn coffee and donuts, *at least*."

I watched Tammy's plum-dark face turn gray behind steam from the coffee urn. "Something's wrong, you guys."

"Why?" asked Paul. "She always complains about the food."

"I don't know why. But be nice, people. Don't slurp, Paul, she hates it. And don't start telling those stories about the porno drive-in up in Danville, Rodney, she thinks it's nasty, even if she does laugh sometimes."

The guys nodded over this—my informed, female opinion

on Tammy, whom they considered strong-headed. Country women were just like that, Rodney had explained to a broken-hearted Paul.

Tammy returned, coffee cup in one hand, and two and a half donuts in the other. When she sat without a smile, Rodney began to joke awkwardly around her:

"The first thing they did to us, at that fat farm, as soon as we got unloaded from the bus, the very *first* thing they did was line us up, and bring out their forceps, and start to poking and measuring at every one of us. You'd've sworn, from the way they'd always be chasing after you with their damn charts and measures, and them *cold* forceps, that they were getting their money out of you by the *pound*, boy, and I only lost fifteen, even after four weeks of that damn hill-running they had us doing..."

Usually Tammy whooped and clapped along with Rodney's stories ("Oh Lordy, Rodney, stop it, b'fore I split.") But today her laughter was muted, and her hands lay still and quiet in her lap.

I yawned and stretched; Rodney and I each smoked another cigarette. "1:37," he announced, consulting his watch.

"Time for me to go hide in the library." I tapped on Tammy's glass. "How about you?"

She swallowed the last of her half-donut, sipped her coffee, wiped her mouth on her napkin. "I don't know. I need to do some studying m'self."

What she needed was a nap, and someone to talk to; maybe me.

Paul and Rodney balled their napkins, collected their glasses and cutlery, and stood to go.

"Bye y'all," she inclined her head.

"Bye Tammy," Paul returned, dropping his hand on her shoulder. She smiled, and patted his wrist.

"Let's go," I urged after they'd left, "It's nice outside."

She nodded and finished her coffee. We put our trays up, and went to sit on the back steps of the Founders' building. Sunny and

3

private, it was one of our favorite spots.

Tammy stretched her legs in front of her, folded her skirt up above her knees, and crossed her hands, palms up, on her lap. She had hands with tapered fingers and muscle-plump palms; hands that grasped so neatly, rested so lightly, I could have known without even being told that they were artist's hands.

I twiddled a stick, hummed a song, waited, while her eyes followed the curve of the thick-rooted pine tree in front of us.

"Two and a *half* donuts?" I ventured.

Her lips curled sheepishly. "I figured two and a half'd be safer than a whole three."

I laughed, and she joined in with a giggle. Carefully, then, I could ask, "So. What is it?"

She glanced at me, at the tree, at the sunlight filtering through its boughs. "My mama's not well."

"Yeah?"

"Daddy called last night to tell me."

Her eyes were deepening in the sun, like clear black pondwater would. She drew her lips in; a corner of her mouth twitched. Oh no, Tammy, I wanted to say, wanting to touch her shoulder. I looked away instead, and waited.

"Mama's sick, and here it was, only last night, that I finally began to realize..." She looked down, curled one set of fingers around a thumb, "...I've been realizing that I might not even *know* her, not like I ought to. My sister Marla was the one raised me, you know."

I hadn't known, not really, and I couldn't now think of a thing to say. I looked down at my feet, and at my empty, cupped-together hands.

But after a few quiet minutes, when she yawned behind her palm, I could suggest a nap. She nodded, and I stood, scuffling my feet to let her know I was leaving. "See ya," I waved. She fluttered her fingers, and drew her eyes back toward the pine tree.

4

****

By suppertime, she was nowhere to be found. None of her suite-mates knew where she was; Rodney had asked. By the next morning, it seemed she had left, because her ancient rusty jeep was gone; I had even stopped by the parking lot to look. A few more meals of no Tammy, and Rodney and I had reached the same conclusion.

"She's done it again," I said. "Left and not told anyone."

Rodney nodded. "Gone and taken that 'fore day creep again." He shook his head. "That girl has some in-dependent ways."

Four days passed without Tammy, and I knew it somehow: her mother was dying. I'd told Paul and Rodney as much at lunch, yet neither had offered any advice. I didn't pray for my friends, I worried instead, knowing even as I did it that worry was even more ineffectual than prayer.

On a Saturday, after five days of no Tammy, I woke up early, looked outside at fresh fall sunlight, and decided I needed a jog. I donned my shorts and t-shirt, laced up my sneakers, and headed out the door, breaking into my paces before I hit the stairwell.

Usually on my morning runs I swung downstairs to Tammy's suite in hopes of bumping into her on her way to breakfast. Today, though, it was her jeep I was looking for, as I shunted down three flights of stairs and loped through the parking lot. And to my surprise, there it was, right in its usual space. But maybe I'd just leave her be until the afternoon, anyway; maybe she'd come to lunch.

But she didn't, and I began to worry again, and wonder: what should I do? Nothing, some part of me said. Do nothing; there is nothing you can do. But I have to, I reasoned; she's my friend. Isn't she?

After lunch, after a half-hour's bout with a mind that refused to read a word of my Norton Anthology, I decided to meander outside. I put the apples and cookies I'd saved from lunch in a bag, and a jazz tape I'd made the night before in my back pocket. Outside, I picked flowers and leaves: wild purple flowers and small red sumac leaves, wrapped inside a swatch of field weed as broad and deeply green as a collard leaf. Artist's colors.

The lounge of Tammy's suite was quiet, and seemed empty; no boogie-thumping radios, no sloshings or flushings from the bathroom down the hall. Everyone's door was closed, except for Tammy's. I slipped across the lounge, raised a hand to knock, and heard a voice, not Tammy's: "Hey. Come on now." It was a voice I'd never heard, though the accent, deeply Southern, was familiar. Goaded beyond all my usual caution, I peeked around the door.

Tammy was sitting on her bed. Her head was down, her hands were folded. Somebody (was it Marla?) was kneeling on the floor, her back to me, her hand on Tammy's knee. "Hey," she repeated, gazing into Tammy's face. But that face was bent so low, I couldn't see it.

"Hey, come on. Hey...Tammy? Sweetie pea?" She reached up to shake Tammy's shoulder; Tammy turned her head away. She hitched over on her knees, grasped both Tammy's arms, shook them. "Now look, baby sister, you've *got* to snap out of this. You've not spoken a word that I've heard in days. And you've *got* to cry, this ain't normal, Tammy. You have not cried a drop that I've seen since you got home, and I can't leave you alone in this nest of snakes with you looking like this."

This nest of *snakes*? I did not belong here. I began to back away, but then my bag hit my knee, and rattled.

When Marla looked around, our eyes met. And she did look like Tammy, I could see, with that part of my mind that remains calm in a crisis: she had the same chin cleft, the same broad, slightly upturned nose. But she was lighter-skinned, and thinner, and naturally not as pretty.

Marla stood, and sucked in her breath, and turned to face me with lips grimly pressed together and hands and arms wrapped protectively around her sister's shoulders. "Tammy? Who is that? Do you know that person?"

Tammy raised her head and turned on me a pair of eyes that were dulled, that were murky with grief. No, she shook her head a little, and brought her eyes back down.

I felt scalded.

"Damn," Marla spat, striding across the room, "Can you tell me why it is that every time you turn around some ofay's got to be up in your face? No sense of decency or privacy, neither."

Why was I standing there? I turned and lunged for the suite door; behind me, Tammy's door slammed.

In my own room, I put my flowers in a glass on the window-sill and sat on my bed, trembling: those eyes, my God, what could *I* hope to do for eyes like that? And why didn't those eyes know me?

"Ain't nothing you can do right now," Rodney answered me that evening. By suppertime, he had the word from Tammy's suitemates: Tammy was in her room, *not* to be disturbed. They were to bring her supper, at her sister's orders, though she herself was insisting that she was not hungry.

"Tammy not hungry? That's bad," I observed. "Is Marla still here?"

Rodney waved his hand. "She's been left."

"An 'ofay' is a foe," I mused. "I looked it up in the diction-ary."

Rodney studied me. "Did someone call you that?"

I nodded. "Marla did. It makes me wonder if Tammy's mother did not exactly 'pass away,' like people say."

"Well you know," he drawled acidly. "She might've not just up and died—she could've been *worked* right into her grave. You ever been down where Tammy's from?"

"She always said it was pretty."

"She wasn't telling you the half of it. It might well be pretty, down that part of the state, but damn scary's what that place is to me, and Reidsville's not black folks' heaven by any means. My ass, fat and soft as it is, might not be alive or in one piece, if I was from a place that rough."

"Bad, huh?"

"*Bad*? They break *backs* down there, girl. Where you think she got those arm muscles you think are so cool?"

"I imagine not from lifting weights."

"Damn straight not. And what about that scar on her sister's arm?"

I wrinkled my forehead. "Didn't notice."

"Tammy never told you?"

"No. Why?"

Rodney shook his head. "Let it drop, girl. If she needs you, you'll know it. If she don't, you'd best stay away. You know how she is."

I swallowed. I couldn't stay away... So maybe I'd wait, just a little bit longer.

Two days later, Tammy emerged from her room, calm and composed, but different. Her chin, always up, now jutted unnaturally. Her shoulders were squared against a weight. She said little, smiled not at all, and still wouldn't stay out for her meals. It was her eyes, though, that made me ache. Once so deep, they looked now as though something had slammed down behind them, blocking out their light. But God, it must have been airless behind there, and hot, and tight, and how could she stand it?

One week passed, and Tammy had not changed; I would sit outside on the library steps and watch her walk straight from the classroom building to our dorm, slowly, with her chin up, as though plowing through a gauntlet. Walking, not even looking around to see if someone, a friend, might be hanging around, watching and waiting.

No more of her laughter, I'd think, sitting alone on the library steps. No more trips to the country in her rattly, rusted jeep, no more listening to her daddy's old gospel records, no more of her sticking her head around my door late at night and asking, eyebrow cocked, "Hey. You got some of them Mars chocolate bars?"

"I can't stand it," I burst out, bringing my fist down on my knee; if nothing else, the loneliness was killing me.

One day later, we happened into each other in the hall in front of her bathroom. I ducked down the stairs, but not before she looked at me, and gave me the inch of opening I needed. She'd looked at me just a second too long, and with a flicker of longing.

So I got up early the next morning, put my toiletries in a plastic bucket, and went downstairs to the second-floor bathroom. I'd done this many times before; the rationale was that my own floor's bathroom was too crowded. The reason, though, was that I'd get to see and talk to Tammy while she picked and dressed her hair, greased her knuckles, knees, and elbows, washed her face and brushed her teeth, and perfumed her neck and wrists.

I swung the bathroom door open, saw that the row of sinks was deserted, and headed for the stalls. I selected one, closed the door, and sat and waited, my pants up and my bucket in my lap. I do know what I'm doing, I reassured myself, and I know why.

The lav door sighed open. A set of feet padded in; the stall door beside me creaked open, then slammed closed. I leaned over; yup, those were Tammy's feet all right. I stood and walked over to the sinks, where I dropped my bucket onto the ledge below the mirrors.

I heard the toilet flush, and slowly soaped my hands. Tammy came around to the sinks, saw me, stiffened, then dropped her bucket nonchalantly at the last sink.

Just the person you wanted to see, I thought grimly. She squeezed some toothpaste on her brush, and began to brush her teeth.

Shit, I moaned; how could I even talk to her with all that

lather in her mouth? She spat into the sink and ran some water. I reached for my pimple cream. She screwed the cap back on her toothpaste, dropped it and the brush into her bucket, then brought out her comb.

Oh Christ, I groaned, she'll take forever with her hair. ("What I need for this knotted-up mess is a *rake*," she'd so often complain.) She'll take forever, and I'll look—and feel—foolish taking fifteen minutes just to brush my teeth. *Now* is the time to do it.

I dropped my pimple cream into my bucket with a clunk. Slowly, I took a step in her direction, and stopped. "Tammy," I commanded. She thrust the comb in her hair, and gripped the edge of the sink ledge with both her hands. Her gaze was fixed straight ahead in the mirror.

I put my hand on her wrist; she pulled away. "Tammy. I don't care if you never want to speak to me again"—(But that wasn't true)—"But the truth is," I began again, "I just can't stand to see you this way. Tammy, have you cried yet?"

She shifted her feet, blinked, said nothing.

"You know, you'll die inside unless you do. You have to let it go, baby."

In my throat, my breath caught: I'd never called anyone "baby" before.

Before she could stop me—before I could stop—I had reached out, drawn her into my arms. Feeling her shoulders go rigid, I stroked the back of her neck. Gently (I was so amazed) gently... I brushed my lips along her cheek, and nuzzled down toward her lips, and kissed her, firmly, on just the corner of her mouth.

I heard a gasp, and a dry sob, and felt her shudder inside my arms.

What am I *doing*, I panicked. ("Snake," someone inside me hissed.) She raised her hands, as though to push me away. (Was that what she wanted to do?) I pulled my arms back, and stepped away in shame, then turned and stumbled out the door, up the steps, and into my room.

Well, I'd done it. I shrugged down into my chair, while my resignation deepened into doubt, then settled into unhappy rationalization: Wasn't passion a part of compassion for a reason?

About two hours later, I remembered my bucket.

Nobody saw her all that day, but passing below her window in the evening, I noticed that her light was on. If her door's open, I resolved, I'll go in. I picked more flowers, went upstairs to my room to roll a joint and wrap up a brownie I'd saved. I put the jazz tape in my back pocket, and went downstairs.

Her suite was dark, but a shaft of yellow light fell across the hall from her open door. I stepped around into the warm cone of light. "Hi," I waved, poised already to turn and go.

She was sitting at her desk beneath her study lamp. She looked up. "Hey Beth." Her face was swollen, her voice thick.

I dropped the brownie and the vase of weeds on a table.

Her face softened. "Thank you sister."

I flushed. "Welcome," I mumbled. "Whatcha doing?"

She turned toward a blank piece of paper. "I'm trying to figure out how to draw her."

I plopped down on her bed. "What'd she look like?"

"She gave me my build, but her complexion's closer to Marla's." Tammy selected a crayon from the tray and laid it on her desk: Dark brown.

"Long hair she pinned down and braided at the sides." She picked another crayon, laid it down: Black.

"Her favorite color to wear was green"—Tammy laid the crayon down—"Except to church, where she always wore white." Tammy lined the crayons up. "And I want to see a blue sky above her head." She picked out the blue, then looked down at the paper.

"I have some music, Tammy. And some smoke." I produced the joint.

She smiled. "Well why you don't light it up then."

11

I struck a match and passed the joint to her. She drew on it, her eyes slit against the smoke.

I put the tape on; a slow, long trumpet filled the shadowed room.

"Yeh," she nodded. "I like that."

We smoked together and fell into silence, me lying back to sneak glances at Tammy's face, at Tammy's eyes intent on the paper that her hands were gently etching.

A few hours later, I was half-asleep and dreaming, while Tammy drew, filling in her mother's face, reaching up every few minutes to catch tears with the heel of her hand.

April Jackson

An Open Letter:

I am a black working class city dyke. When I decided to go to college, I got more than I bargained for. I decided upon a small catholic primarily women's college 30 miles away from Pittsburgh simply because they were willing to foot most of my bill. I had not anticipated being the single black face in a class, one of two in a lecture hall or even one of 20 or so in a thousand. I also had not anticipated meeting, befriending and falling in love with a smalltown white girl from the Pennsylvania Dutch side of the tracks.

Amy was the face that respected my differences when others were trying to ignore them. Amy was the friend that encouraged me to use the rage that spat out passion to my advantage and write. Amy held me as I cried, angry with administrators, staff and the world at large for not respecting the energy I put into my beliefs. Amy understood, even though she did not experience first hand, the pain, frustration and anger that is at the center of my life. Together we surpassed all of that to reach an understanding that the ego of a relationship is fragile. That regardless of your political affiliation, economic status, personal life, etc., etc.... being a lesbian in love is a dangerous thing.

13

Another Open Letter:

I had a startling revelation
a few days ago:
I
am this judeo-christian,
capitalist
western country's
alter ego.

By being
alive
angry
articulate
loud
rude
brash
me
I am a super power's worst enemy.

I have often prided myself
on being somewhat
of a radical,
but being
this society's nightmare
is more than I could have hoped for.

Just by being
black
female
lesbian
I live on the edge.

Sacred Games

we are not sacred nor are we polite.

we are   sunday mornings   sprawled in 9 am light   laughing
with the church bells   warm   wild-haired   earlobes and breasts
funky and naked   with books berry tea and the crumbs of
something   crunchy-sweet   and breakfast like

we are   musky odors   steamed windows   heavy breathing
buttons zippers hooks eyes redness swelling and veins
limbs thrown torsos mingling creme atop coffee brandy over
ice   teeth   hair   nails   spit rolling   gliding
                            up and
                                mmmmmmmmmmmmm......
        colors bouncing off the roof of the car

we are grasping groping crawling loving crying haunted
hating   and afraid   but we are making it and we are not yet
                        insane.

Elizabeth Clare

Think Twice Before You Call Me Courageous Again

Glass walls. For the first six weeks of my life, I lived in an incubator. I would scoot myself into a corner, jamming my head against the glass wall, and scream until a nurse moved me. My parents watched from the door of the preemie ward. They didn't hold me until I was four weeks old. Early on, a nurse told them, "You can always tell which ones will live. Your baby, she's a fighter. She'll live."

I didn't walk until I was two or talk until I was three. So when I was two-and-a-half, my parents took me to Fairview State Hospital to find out what was "wrong" with me. In flashes I remember: long corridors, white medical coats, lying on a long, cold table, dressed in a tissue paper gown, so afraid of falling off, so afraid of what the man bending over me might do. As a result of this testing, they told my parents that I was "dull normal to retarded." A couple years later when it was apparent that I wasn't "retarded," Grandma told me, "God made you smart to make up for your handicap."

Age twelve, I went to the Crippled Children's Division for more tests, and we finally learned that I had cerebral palsy. Until then, my family didn't know what caused my shaking or lack of coordination. My parents always said that I had a handicap, a word I thought they had created specifically to describe me. I can still hear the silence in that room after the physical therapist said the words *cerebral palsy*.

But I don't want this to be a memory piece where I put my life into chronological order. I didn't have the words *cerebral palsy* until I was twelve or the word *ableism* until a few years ago. What do those words mean? Where does honesty lie now that the silence is riding its way out?

For years the words *brave, courageous,* and *inspirational* filled that silence. I sit here staring at my face in the night-black window, trying to explain those three words. All my life, while I've written poetry, run on my high school cross country team, worked as a political organizer, walked across the country with the Great Peace March, people—both men and women, lesbians included—have called me brave, courageous, or inspirational simply because I have CP. In response, I tell them: I simply live in the body I was born into and do the things I want/need to do just as anyone does. I tell them: I don't much believe in courage. I tell them: I hate to be patronized. Or I am silent, smile politely. When I do speak, I always wonder if anyone really hears me. Most people end up trying to hide their discomfort behind very set and determined definitions of *courage, bravery,* and *inspiration.* In doing so, they never see me as a peer but as someone who has "overcome her handicap."

When I think of the word *overcome,* I think of the years I spent avoiding mirrors and my reflection in night-black windows. I didn't want to be reminded of my hands, which don't bend smoothly or move with any grace. I wished to be—or at least appear—"normal," meaning people wouldn't stare in restaurants, banks, grocery stores, meaning I wouldn't have to ask for more time on timed tests because I write very slowly, meaning I wouldn't have to explain why my hands tremble, why I talk slowly, don't enunciate clearly. One day I wished I could cut off my right arm so it wouldn't shake. Overcoming is amputation.*

When I think of the word *overcome,* I think of a story my mother tells: when I was a year old, Grandma came from Michigan to take care of the family while Mom recovered from a kidney

---

* After I wrote this line, I started to think about people who have had limbs amputated and how for them amputation must mean something entirely different, possibly akin to what CP means to me.

operation. Every afternoon Grandma tried to rock me to sleep. I would cry and wrestle to get off her lap, but she insisted on holding me. After weeks of this, I finally let her rock me. I clearly see myself as that little girl's inheritor, not letting anyone hold me until I can't resist the comfort anymore. To be held means letting another person feel my shaking, the way tension rises with the shaking, and how it locks into my back, shoulders, and right arm. Sometimes the tension is worse when people touch me. Somewhere I learned that I had to hide the shaking, to pass in the world and to myself. Now I want to learn how not to pass, how to crack the glass wall. Overcoming is living behind that glass wall.

When I think of the word *overcome*, I think of a day when I was nine and stood in the playground surrounded by playmates. They taunted me, "Monkey, retard, weirdo." I couldn't do anything, couldn't convince them I wasn't, couldn't run fast enough to get away from them. Finally my father came along, and the kids scattered, leaving me to my tears, to the feeling of being a monkey. I didn't let anyone comfort me. Overcoming is telling this story so matter-of-factly that I forget how my nine-year-old self felt.

But more recently something else has happened with the word *courageous* that is totally unconnected to the word *overcome*. Able-bodied women whom I love and respect have called me courageous, and I have listened, maybe because they're listening to me, not just to my disability or their own discomfort. From my journal:

> 1/20—Still at WomanShare. A thing from yesterday: that man who came looking for the Johnsons while M and I were alone in the main house, he was obviously lost and needed directions. He couldn't/wouldn't understand me; each time I spoke to him, he'd turn to M and ask her to repeat

what I had just said, basically asking her to translate for him. M refused, telling him to ask me. Later she came up to my cabin, and we talked for a long time, dykely talk, more about being allies, what it means for her to be able-bodied in the face of my disability. There is a part of me that is overwhelmed by her listening and noticing. When I talk to her about ableism, I begin to see my own growing honesty and understanding. To explore my self-doubt, to call it self-doubt, to hear M say, "I think he was discounting you," to hear her talk about moving away from the word *handicap*, all amazes me.

I have accepted the word *courage* from M.

I wonder why her listening feels so new and unfamiliar, and then I remember high school. I ran long distance on the track and cross country teams. I was a slow, stubborn runner who placed last in many races but never quit. After these races, complete strangers would tell me how brave or inspirational I was, hugging me, putting an uninvited arm around me, occasionally patting my head. Some of these invasions left me in tears, not knowing what to do or how to react. When I would come home, still upset, my parents would tell me that I had to accept people's "compliments." This answer always made me unsettled, angry, knowing that they weren't listening, that no one really listened. But I could never explain. I grew to believe I half-deserved the patronizing, no matter how invasive it felt. In the end, my discomfort became my own personal problem rather than a reaction to someone else's ableism.

There are days now that stand in contrast to those years, days full of listening. Last week I ate dinner with a friend who probably knows pieces of this story as well as I do. As usual, our conversation turned to the politics of being a Black, able-bodied lesbian and a white, disabled lesbian in this world. She had a couple stories about racism, and I, a couple about ableism. They weren't new or unusual stories but ones that we don't tell often. I was telling her about a woman who had called me "dear" but so clearly meant "cripple." My friend said, "You could easily insert the word *nigger* there." Somehow we started laughing hysterically at the thought of "dear nigger, dear cripple." Neither word is funny, but we both knew exactly what the other meant.

As I tell the stories and watch women listening, sometimes laughing and other times crying, the cracks in the glass wall grow. I begin to look steadily at ableism and learn not to pass. My father once said in a restaurant as people stared at me, "It is their problem, not yours." He was right and still is, but my answer then was to pretend the staring didn't exist, which meant I could pretend that I didn't have CP, that I was "normal." Now I am learning to stare right back at those people, not hiding my hands, until they stop calling me a courageous cripple with their eyes or until they ask me an honest question. I can't do it every time, but I've come a long way from the girl who pretended to be "normal" while quietly and unconsciously absorbing all the stares. I want the glass wall to shatter.

But passing is also about my own discomfort, not just other people's. Lying with a new lover after making love, my right arm begins to tremble, and I pull away, trying to stop the shaking, so she won't feel it. Tension rises through my arm and shoulder. I don't know what this able-bodied woman thinks of my body, of the trembling, of my hands that don't travel smoothly over her body. I want to hide, to pass yet again. Then she turns to me and asks, "What does the trembling feel like?" She asks this as she has asked many questions in the past three days. Her words push at the glass wall, telling me, "I can see through this wall, but I want more. I want to be on the other side with you." To answer her will take a long time, but I want to begin. Later she says, "I like your hands when they tremble over me. It feels good, like extra touching." The glass wall has shattered; the splinters will demand my attention later, but for the moment let me remember that passing isn't even functional here. If I pass, or even try, I do so because of my discomfort, not hers.

In the end, not passing means telling the truth, wearing myself, a lesbian with cerebral palsy, as strongly as I can. If there is any courage in me, it isn't in what I do but in living with the words *courageous cripple*. It is a daily, ordinary kind of courage that includes laughing, raging, and loving the women who listen.

Jodi

Loving In Spite of Mistakes

Those moments when your innards lurch—how could I have done that? And also the ones where you think: how COULD she DARE??? I love learning. But I hate being educated. I love being really understood. But I hate having to explain. It always seems that once the need for lecture has occurred, the trust has been violated. Either I've blown it or she has. I may never do it again, she may have really learned her lesson, but it's too late.

Or is it? I can think of wimmin who I've argued with and still loved. I can think of errors I've made and the relationship survived. I can think of plenty of times I've taken criticism, learned my lesson, carried it with me into the world—as well as times I have explained something and not borne a grudge about it. I've yelled my head off without resentment, too.

I think that's part of it. If I can yell and scream and express my full rejection of her statement or behavior, and she can take it in and stay open and honest with me, then it'll be okay. If I can blow it and she can tell me how I've hurt her, and I can stay with that and feel it and respond... if we trust and love each other... if we're real...

And if it's not too boring. If it's not the same shit over and over, all the time, if the "issue" doesn't take up too much space in the relationship... If I haven't suddenly discovered that *everyone* in my life betrays me here, if it's just one day in one relationship where I deal with this and not my entire life... if I don't leave it all to her to figure out... If we notice when we've blundered... If we correct it right away...

If we can deal with both behavior *and* with feelings...

If you think it's difficult or expensive or overwhelming to

make access happen as a non-disabled person, just imagine how hard it is for a disabled womon living without access.

If you think it's painful being told that what you did was racist, just imagine how it feels to be the target of your actions.

I have been afraid with other wimmin. Afraid a failure in my consciousness would yawn open between us, and damage would be done. I have found in my own life that when someone has one of those gaps around *my* issues, I expect them to change, and they rarely do.

The fear of saying something that can't be taken back... I've been on the other end of this as well. It's dreadful. When she says something and I get that feeling like being punched in the stomach, and that heart squeezing shut, slam, smack... then silence. What makes it so? What makes something like that final?

When I think back on examples, either way (no matter who's at fault), I think it comes from not believing it is really worth it to continue. Lack of faith in the other womon, the relationship, her commitment to the issue. Lack of willingness to grow. Forgetting that it's important. Oh, hell, I'm so much more aware than half the world, why bother? If she'll never love me anyway, if I can never make up for all the rest of history, what difference does it make? I'm just one person, my work will never have an impact...

I have felt a need to wipe out poverty. To mediate the crisis in the Middle East. I have become enraged at diets, clothing, seats and turnstiles, wanted to crash through prisons, I have needed to end estrangements between peoples. And it's this very urgency that stalls me. IF ONE MORE WOMON SUFFERS... I won't be able to go on.

And so it's time to re-empower myself. To remember what I

ask of others. I have many friends who haven't wiped out poverty. Wimmin I love, adore, admire who have not solved the crisis in the Middle East. The world is not accessible. I can put out information, make demands, create spaces, interrupt the litanies of hatred. I can write letters to offensive people in authority, and try to encourage my friends to eat. It does seem paltry. There are so many projects to be done.

What do I ask of others, on *my* issues? Interest, growing levels of awareness, an openness of spirit. I want them to read and think about our literature. I want them to educate each other, speak up in public places, feel and act as if it matters, and not think they're doing me a favor.

I want some non-disabled dyke to start a newsletter titled *Practicing Anti-Ableism.* I want everyone to be enthused to read it and write for it. I want non-Jews and non-Crips to be outraged about anti-Semitism and ableism and to speak up, to separate and focus on alternatives. I want a few to try to change the system and most to work outside it. I want to know that everything we do comes out of love instead of guilt. I want to be able to trust again that no one's revolution will exclude me, and that never again will we have one-way coalitions.

I am very angry about all the people—and I mean lesbians in particular—who really get it about one issue and forget about the rest. Anti-oppression work, social change, community building, liberation is not about the few being assimilated to the many. It's about a truth for all of us, that our issues overlap. It's fine to work especially on one issue, but you have to know and care about the rest, or at least be open to hearing about them when someone tries to tell you. Racism in the disability rights movement, inaccessible womon of color spaces, classism, ageism, alienation against "crazy" people... Do you think there are no disabled dykes of color? No young or old dykes with radical ideas? Perhaps that

Jews don't die of our oppression? That you can escape the effects of this on all wimmin?

I think that all real changing comes from caring, from sincerely wanting to embrace the possibilities. I'm not saying that it's easy after that, but without it you might as well despair. What hurts me most is when I approach another lesbian and offer to help make something happen and she still has some resistance or excuse. Like all the periodicals who won't cooperate with making themselves available on tape. All the wimmin who say they're so busy working on their own issues that they just can't take it in about fat, or Jews. This resistance to even *believing* in the *existence* of oppressions has simply got to go. We have to realize that awareness of others doesn't have to mean we de-emphasize our own concerns. It's that same concept of divide and conquer, which keeps us struggling away in isolation, division, horizontal hostility. We're stuck with a system that has rot and cruelty at its core until we get the underlying concept that liberation needs to be the center, sisterhood and non-alienation the *principle*, of the present, for the future. It feels good to be an ally. When any of us strives toward freedom, we should *all* rejoice, cooperate, and give encouragement.

I think that adding a little bit more love and sweetness to our motivations would go a long way towards putting us more into the clear. And lesbians are the best ones to do this. No one becomes a lesbian out of guilt. It's loving wimmin that makes it happen. And that is true for all good things that happen in my world.

Susan Stinson

Thin Friends' Pantoum

We are falling away from fat as a topic.
You know my pride in my breasts as blubber flowers.
We laugh at the ones who say they don't notice.
You hear me speak of the whale's powerful tongue.

You know my pride in my breasts. Blubber flowers
with stretch marks that color, then glisten.
You hear me speak with the whale's powerful tongue.
You give a thin nod: expansive ways of being.

Stretch marks color, then glisten.
You blush half through your diet story.
You give a thin nod. Expansive ways of being
must not include growing out of your clothes.

You blush half through your diet story,
then change the words to "eating healthy,"
trying not to include growing out of your clothes
as a reason you are leaving bread for lettuce.

Just change the words to "eating healthy."
We'll play dumb enough to miss the implications.
The reasons you are leaving bread for lettuce
never touch your attitudes about my body.

We play dumb enough to miss the implications.
We laugh at the ones who say they notice.
We never touch your attitudes about my body
and fall away from fat as a topic.

Overnight

We can't overlap. Your body firms
against my belly.
The sky light squirms

with flies hovering awake. Shall we
wake to look? Your head keeps the crack
between the pillows. I am a whale. See

my breasts tucked up a slit in my fat,
my subtle muscles, my lack of grace
on land. Your breasts remark on onions, a sack

of which becomes my paunch.
You tense. I launch.

Swim

The pond is green.
Gracious skin
and fat, my breasts
rise to the surface.

You dive
past the bottle glass.
Dense-bodied, muscled
you struggle in water
but crave   the shock of it.

I loosen my feet,
lean back: corpulent
and perfect naked
under such hot sun.

Pam Mitchell

That Great Divide

"Loving across class differences." I struggle to provide this notion with an appropriate container with neat definition, politeness, the preeminence of the rational—in other words, to make it a middle-class thing. I'm sure I'm capable of producing yet another neat little essay about class within a political framework. I've done it a dozen times before, utilizing just the "right" amount of that ability to distance and abstract that I learned so well at those middle-class universities I went to on financial aid, while at the same time remembering to draw on my personal experience because that's the way good middle-class feminists say to do it. The pieces I've written in the past have gotten me into trouble. Some have uncharitably called them "diatribes." I've learned the hard way: my feminist sisters welcome anger as long as it's directed at the system and at men. Just don't let it hit too close to home.

But "attitude" from members of my community is not the only thing that makes it feel like a challenge to keep these words within the margins. The problem is that there is no way to put "love" and "class" in the same essay and have the pieces line up. A discourse on "loving" requires embracing tenderness, vulnerability, connection. Its raw material is relationships with real women I've tried to love and who've tried to love me back. Our failures are in no small measure due to finding ourselves on different tiers of a system of class oppression that we're each committed to destroying.

"Class" is about the antithesis of love: division, hierarchy, exploitation. It's hard to write about my experiences of love mediated and mangled by class without hurting these women with whom I've struggled so hard, whom I've loved so imperfectly. Class made my need and my bitterness a vein running through our relationship, as inseparable from us as was their resentment, their guilt, their pity. If the particular women I'm thinking of read this and recognize themselves, I hope they realize that I'm saying we gave it our best shot, despite the class system that divides us.

Sometimes I've lost sight of that mean class monster, perceiving the limitations it has imposed upon us as faults of my own and hating myself for them. At other times I've blamed it all on those "higher"-class folks, feeling venomous toward them and hating myself for that. In my uglier moments the very concept of "loving across class difference" strikes me as an oxymoron, a logical and practical impossibility. The class divide is always there. At times it takes a shape more mocking than monstrous, a fun-house mirror reflecting me back as grotesque failure, too angry, too disorganized, too shameful to compete, to be seen or appreciated or loved.

Is it my choice to spend my time wrestling with this class demon? In a sense, I've "chosen" to abandon my own kind. I do low-paying clerical work like both my parents did and live in a working-class neighborhood, yet I have nothing to do with my family of origin. Nor do the people I "hang with" now have much in common with the people I grew up with. My "chosen" family is a community of lesbian-feminist activists who are careerists in movement jobs or social services or the arts. Working-class women compose only a small number of the women who have managed to fit themselves into this circle, and those who are working class keep a low profile and have assimilated to some extent.

Though dominated by white, highly-educated women from middle and upper-class backgrounds, this subculture reflects back to me much of the identity I've embraced—my politics, my values, my interests. The raw material for this present-day "self" is certainly the person I was raised as. It includes my political way of looking at the world, my faith in the printed word, attributes that come from my mother and her mother and are certainly fed by Eastern European Jewish cultural traditions that historically have cut across class lines. More than some other peoples, Jewish poor and working-class people carry with us a history of activism and visionary dreams of social change, while among even the poorest Jews (at least the poorest of male Jews), reading and education have been respected activities not entirely reserved for the leisure classes. But nonetheless, I emerged from several years of upper-middle-class-defined university and Left countercultural life profoundly altered, with a new self-image and a new aesthetic out of synch with the lifestyle I was born into, yet unprepared for the economic upward mobility to go with it. My degree in anthropology from an alternative college hasn't done a whole lot for me.

For the most part, the members of this tribe I've "chosen" as family whom I know best and love the most are Jews, because Jewish women are a kind of home for me. Though a few come from backgrounds similar to mine and continue to struggle financially, most have been and continue to be relatively affluent. They've traded in some of the privilege that is their birthright for the chance to do work they consider meaningful, and are often quick to point out this sacrifice. Still, they earn more than most working people, including me. And they maintain the crazy-making hidden access: the unacknowledged shots of wealth that arrive from family whenever they're needed, and often when they're not.

My continual contact with this sector of the Jewish population leaves me struggling with historically-dangerous stereotypes: that Jews come with money, that even those not born rich are smart enough to figure out a way to make up for it by selling their brains for a good price. Although I know this is a lie reinforced by the invisibility of other working-class Jews, part of me believes it and tries to understand why I am the exception. Is it the *shiksa* blood on my father's side, the absence of a family I can build on, some tragic character flaw?

When I've been in need, these friends and lovers have often been there to "help me out." (I wonder, are they willing to do so because of Jewish values, Jewish guilt?) The edges of my otherwise essentially impoverished existence have been smoothed by their gifts, their ingenious income-sharing plans, their strategic bail-outs. If not for them, I couldn't own my little piece of a limited-equity co-op apartment building, couldn't have taken various vacations when I desperately needed them, wouldn't have had the money to live on when I could barely work after I was sexually victimized, the cash to make the payment when a defaulted college loan caught up with me.

But there are corrosive side-effects. I accept with gratitude these "perks," but not without the feelings of worthlessness that come with saying "I need." I can't help but experience this as a shortcoming, can't avoid those shameful moments when I've wondered whether I might be hanging on to a bad relationship just to keep the benefits coming.

And then there's *their* guilt, their judgment, their resentment of me for triggering these unwanted feelings. To them, my financial need must sometimes feel like a bottomless pit. I'm not allowed to have other needs or flaws, as though financial need is a character defect: so-and-so has a bad temper, such-and-such isn't always honest, G. is always broke. Real or imagined, these judgments are forever ringing in my ears, making me feel hatred for the folks I love.

My first woman lover went to Radcliffe, so obviously she was better than me (my own assessment, not hers). Then came one from another Ivy League school, and then another. Since all three are still in my life, let's call them Mesdames X and Y and Z for the sake of anonymity. Each of them is very Jewish-identified, although they grew up as very different kinds of Jews. Each seemed like a peer while we were involved, dressing as I did, renting apartments similar to mine, finding makeshift work in the same ways that I did. Yet the differences determined by accident of birth have become more apparent over time and were present in subtle ways when we were together. For example, while I was with Y, she was the one who owned a car. The same has been true for every lover I've been with. In virtually every case, familial financial input has made these cars possible. I've owned two cars in my 39 years. One was an ancient clunker that died less than a year after it was given to me by a wealthy friend. I sobbed as I watched the guy from Bucky's Auto Parts tow away my mobility, my little part in a world where people own and control things. The other car, my only inheritance when my father dropped dead suddenly while in a state of bankruptcy, was equally decrepit. I owned it for a matter of hours; I never did get that damned old shitbox to start.

X, Y and Z all have professional careers now, though these are sometimes precarious and sometimes they feel ambivalent about them. Each hated graduate school but blundered through it anyhow, with considerable parental support. On the other hand, I literally hitched a ride cross-country to begin a doctoral program with no resources save the pack on my back and a few promises from the financial aid office. I dropped out when the money dried up after nine months of intolerable alienation. I couldn't see going any deeper in debt to support their futile attempts to mould me into their kind of back-slapping/back-stabbing professional. My reward for quitting has been, of course, the promise of the different, more interminable alienation of low-paid menial labor.

After we broke up, X's parents helped her buy a two-family house. That she had either the resources or the audacity to buy something that big and permanent blew me away. This purchase elicited one of the many instances when my class rage has kindled responses I'm not proud of. I heard about it while X and I were taking a six-month breather from one another immediately following our breakup. But when we kept running smack into each other that year at Gay Pride, X finally tired of our ignoring each other and approached me, reaching out to take my hand in hers. I shoved it aside and stomped away, spitting, "I don't shake hands with landlords."

In subsequent years, Y and Z each purchased condos with their parents' money shortly after our relationships ended. By that time I'd gotten used to the idea that some people grow up with ownership as a "but of course."

These women and those from similar backgrounds often don't even recognize that nearly everything in U.S. culture in general and in our particular feminist subculture reinforces the idea that their experience is the norm. When I was first getting to know Y, for example, she told me her father built the house she lived in growing up in an affluent suburb. Naively, I thought of the carpenters waiting for work-calls at the union hall where my father worked as a clerk throughout my childhood. I pictured her father in workclothes with hammer and two-by-fours on the weekends. I knew he worked as an academic and consultant during the week. She later took me to see the place, wanting to share it with me although she was nervous that when I saw it I might have what we jokingly called a "class attack." It turned out to be a gorgeous expanse of redwood with a stream running through it, the kind of tasteful, unadorned natural beauty that smells to me (not unpleasantly) like crisp new dollar bills. I realized that "building" such a place must have meant not hammering every nail but hiring the designers and contractors. I did experience a "class attack" of shame that day, induced not by the opulence of the place but, rather, by the awareness that someone with whom I was so intimate could be entirely oblivious to the working assumptions of my working-class mind. My shame was so virulent that I never even broached the subject of our radically different operating definitions of the basic verb "to build."

Years of struggle, persistent financial need, and my insistence on framing discussion in terms of class have pushed my affluent associates to join my struggle to redefine other words: "fair," for example, and "to share." At times we've thought we've reached a workable definition of these concepts, only to have it fall flat when we've put it into practice. One time, for example, I was unemployed and broke and Z was living comfortably on her paycheck while dividend checks from her trusts were accumulating in the bank. She didn't feel okay about giving me money outright. She had already spent a fair amount of money on me, and didn't want to feel she was being taken advantage of or had to buy my love. On the other hand, I couldn't see borrowing the money and then struggling to make payments that would simply land in her bank, unneeded and untouched. We decided her money would be a loan, but my payments would not go back to her but to a particular granting organization that funded feminist projects, with her matching them dollar for dollar. But after I landed a part-time clerical job, I could not bring myself to write monthly checks to an organization that funded groups consisting of people who were in no more need than I was. Our idea made perfect sense from one angle, yet in the bigger picture it made no sense at all.

I wonder whether writing this piece can help make sense out of that bigger picture, whether I've accomplished what I set out to do. I wanted to write about how fucking hard it is to come from a different class background from nearly everyone in my life. I wanted to write about how hard it is always scrounging for money while those around me don't have to worry so much. I wanted to write about how much I hate having to feel grateful, beholden to people for sharing with me what comes to them with so little effort and doesn't come to me. I wanted to write about how I secretly hate them all a good percentage of the time and feel like I'm using them and feel like maybe I'm entitled to use them; about how I sometimes feel incapable of loving because there is such a damned deficit, some of which comes from lack of love and lack of self-esteem and not from material deprivation. Sometimes it's so hard to figure out where the line is. I wanted to write about the abyss, the love I feel and the impossibility of building bridges that can cut across my anger, my self-loathing, my shame, my fear, my exhaustion. I wanted to write about how I wish it didn't always feel like it's *my* job or the job of others like me—other working-class dykes who already have enough work to do—to point out to our privileged friends and comrades that the abyss is there, that some of us are on the other side of it, and that it shouldn't be us who get stuck doing all the hard labor of building the bridges across that great divide.

Lois Van Houten

To a Lover/Twenty Years Younger

You're my 'going in' place…
I'm your 'jumping off' place.
You're my going back place
I'm your going forward.
With you, I'm twenty years ago:
with me, you chart your star-trek
years ahead.
You take off from my compass
northerly position.
I arrow into myself/from your south.
I swing from the monkey bars with
you inside me.
You climb about on the mountain peaks
without me.
I grope the jungle/in my pith helmet:
you rap signals on your hard-hat with
an icicle.
I call to you from my steaming pit:
"I'm here, I'm here."
You yodel down/you just want to see
over the next ridge.

Giving Quarter

I won't fight you anymore.
I won't pluck apples from
your tree and pelt you with them.

I won't play my flute and charm
the worm from the pit.

I'm old and this magician's hair
grows white with snow though
underneath its arctic cap   the
fire still crests.

I'll wait until the obsidian of
your rage/cools to a workable calm:
then, with my lapidary skill I'll
fashion a stone to swing as an
amulet between my breasts.

Just to **remind** me.

Sandra Lambert

Disability and Intimacy

Journal Entries

4-22-83   I went to the movies with Eleanor last night. It was about a high school girl with cerebral palsy who wants to be a cheerleader. It brought back memories of the kids in elementary school yelling at me as I walked down the hall. And the girl in high school that called me "crip." And I convinced myself that she was saying "creep" affectionately. I was new in the school and was so glad for someone to notice me, talk to me. I feel degraded thinking about it.

4-23-83   I'm almost finished with *Zami* and I just read about Audre pouring boiling water over her hands because she was in a rage at her lover and didn't know how to express it. She wanted to murder so instead she mutilated herself. I remembered when I lived on Drexel Ave. and was very low, lying in bed and thinking of going in the kitchen, boiling a pot of water and pretending to accidentally pour it over my feet. Then people would have to take care of me, then they would notice how miserable I was. I went through the process in my mind of actually step-by-step how I would do it over and over again. But I never did it. I was afraid of the pain. I always thought of this as the depths of self pity, but Audre makes me think of rage as a reason too. What does it mean that she, a writer, burns her hands and I want to burn my legs and feet? Is it because I thought of them as useless and easy to sacrifice? Is it because they were the site of so much other pain?

7-23-85   My first morning alone in my new tent. I was uneasy and scared of the dark when I came over after dinner last night. I got in bed and started to read trash science fiction in order to distract myself, but the night just outside my screen door kept pulling on my attention. The moon was a few days past new and low in the sky, just below the treeline. As the wind picked up and shook the trees I could catch glimpses of her through the layers and layers of foliage that are on my West. The moon, criss crossed by swaying branches, was broken into pieces of golden sparkles, sparkles that were moonlight, amazingly strong, that made shifting sparkle shadows inside my tent. It was a blessing. And closer to the screen were smaller pieces of the moon, fireflies. I put the book down and really accepted all the noises and shadows and felt at peace as I fell asleep. This morning I woke up to the early sun shining in my back window streaming directly onto my altar scarf. A lizard just scurried over the roof and window. It's safe here, and beautiful, and comfortable.

    While I'm here I'm going to try to write of my memories of early childhood, especially around hospitalization and disability. This is my first writing. Where do I begin? Just do it. Plunge in.

    I remember being scared one time when my parents came to take me for a visit when I was at Warm Springs Polio Foundation. I was on a stretcher and we were in one of those majestic hallways and they were laughing with other parents and having a good time and I was petrified. I knew we would be late getting back to the ward and she, the head nurse, would be very, very angry. I was terrified out of my mind. I think I tried to tell my parents that we would be late, but they said it wouldn't matter, not to worry. I knew better, but I didn't know what else to do and just lay in misery until they took me back. I think this woman, the nurse, read the riot act to my parents but I'm not sure. In fact, all of this is very hazy. But I remember the feeling of being caught between two authority systems and not able to do anything. A feeling of it being unusual and precious for my parents to sit and laugh, but that enjoyment shut me out. I couldn't relax and be part of it because someone had to be aware of the rules.

This woman, the nurse, I don't remember her name except that there was one nurse we called Miss Banana. But I don't know if this is her or even if all these memories are of the same woman. But I'll call her all one person until I can tell different. All I have right now are these fragments. Are they real at all?

I remember her standing over me with enema preparations and me thinking of it as punishment because I couldn't shit on my own.

I remember a dream, one I've had many times since the hospital, but not in 10 or 15 years, of going to hell. Of being bad, not following the rules, and so going to a hell of red devils with tails.

I know that there was more to it but I can't remember.

I remember hating having my nose cleaned with Q-tips in the hospital. I feel shame even now.

I remember lying in bed, not on the ward, it must have been just after surgery in the recovery room, and feeling something wet in my left groin. I was sure I had peed on myself and was scared to tell anyone. The nurse came and on a routine check saw that my incision had opened. Then they took me into a big, cavernous room and a man (the doctor?) told me all about the thread they were using to sew it back up. I don't remember any pain and I rather enjoyed the attention and explanations.

No one ever seemed to understand how scared I was.

7-24-85   I've been reading *Mother Wit* and I've started doing some of the breathing exercises. I get sort of panicked when I try to be conscious about my breathing—like I don't get enough oxygen or I won't do it right.

My memories—do I have any more? I need to use dreaming to access them.

I remember having a cowgirl outfit— fringe, hat, holster, guns. I crawled around the yard in it. There were other kids—was I playing with them? Fragments.

I remember a little cart or wagon that I could make go with my hands by pushing something up and down. I loved it!

I remember seals and a cave, wet and

dripping. Being carried on my father's shoulders with the echoing sounds of the seals. I couldn't have been more than two years old.

I remember being fitted for a back brace— 10 years old? I was naked with men pulling and stretching me while the mold was put on. Smiling, joking faces leaning over me pulling in all directions. It felt good to be touched and I wondered when it would start hurting.

I remember having a cast from my chest down to my toes and it was curved. When I lay on my stomach my feet and head were up in the air and I could rock. They called me Elvis Presley. My mother would reach her hand between the cast with its crumbling plaster and my always damp back and she would scratch.

It's been another morning in my tent. The day is beautiful after a night of lightning and thunder and wind and rain. Last night the canvas walls snapped and shook and I slept deeply, feeling safe in the middle of a storm.

It feels dangerous to me to share these journal entries and write about disability and intimacy without knowing that you, the reader, have a political context within which to react. It's important you know that disability is not a personal misfortune, that it is a form of oppression, an oppression firmly institutionalized into our social, economic, and spiritual systems. Without such an analysis, perhaps even with one, these memories might elicit pity or a guilty flinching away, and the way guilt and pity manifest in the world is very dangerous to me. They threaten my health, my economic security, and my options for love and caring. But within a political context these examples of pain, shameful feelings, and vulnerability can become strong, clearly defined realizations of the effects of oppression in our most intimate lives.

What role does physical disability play in the development and maintenance of intimacy? Or, how do I find friends and lovers?

On the most obvious level, I have to be able to go where the girls are—for me that means to dances, political meetings, to women's bookstores. I need to be able to mingle. Each time an event is inaccessible, my chance of making friends is decreased on a simple statistical basis. So I mingle and subsequently meet a few lesbians. How do I get to know them better? Unless lust jumps in and rushes intimacy, what often happens among more able-bodied lesbians are spontaneous events. They go to grab something to eat after a dance. They need to drop some leaflets off and end up staying to talk for awhile. I am often cut off from these events. I'm too tired to go out after a dance. I can't get up the steps to a new acquaintance's house, so I have a friend drop off the leaflets and she gets to visit, not me. It's hard to figure out what to do. How do I continue to feel powerful in these situations and not get stuck in loneliness and self-pity? I sometimes know how and have the energy to access anger, turn it into action, and make loud public demands that meetings and social events be made accessible, but I can't really think of a way to mount a viable campaign against inaccessible spontaneous happenings.

Anyway, I make a new friend, or become part of a social community of lesbians, or begin to feel that sense of "lover potential" in someone. If that someone is an able-bodied lesbian, a dynamic that can develop early on is that she and I have a physical interaction because I need some kind of help. This physical interaction is not necessarily based on trust, sexual attraction, or even affection as it would be in a developing relationship between two able-bodied lesbians. So I'm unsure.

Does that supporting touch on my shoulder mean she thinks I'm the hottest thing around, or is she simply being a well-trained girl scout doing her good deed for the day? In my life I have made the wrong assumption in both directions.

New friends and I don't get to be casual for very long. Right off we have issues to deal with that are not at all subtle. I have a group of friends for dinner but most of them can't reciprocate... one lives up a hellacious flight of stairs, the other down a steep gravelly driveway. In restaurants she is asked what I want to eat by the waiter. Or people on the street ask if you are sisters, even if she's six foot tall with blond hair and I'm 4'10" and a brunette. I've finally decided this means they don't think she's with you out of free choice.

Time passes and I become intimate with a lesbian, as a lover, a friend, or perhaps we develop a good working relationship. She becomes part of my life, my family. She's one of the reasons I have for getting up in the morning. How does ableism affect these more intimate relationships? I'd like to begin an answer with three scenarios from my life. Please remember that these events have been greatly simplified. In other words, they are not all of the truth.

I used to drink coffee. Just in the mornings usually, and my favorite cup was the first one, especially if I could have it while I was still in bed. But since I couldn't get it without putting my braces on, which meant taking a bath first and then putting on clothes, the whole feeling of being newly awake and sipping on coffee was ruined—unless someone got it for me. I lived with my lover, Margaret, and a friend, Judy, at the time and often they would make me a cup. I really liked it and told them so. Well, the years went by and at some point I began to get the feeling that perhaps getting my coffee was no longer something my lover loved to do for me. I checked it out many times and finally she said that yes, she had come to really dislike that chore and had for some time.

Another example. I was living by myself at this time and Sherry, my lover, said "Let me take out your garbage." I said, "No, no, no. I could take out my own trash." She said she knew that, but it was no big deal for her to take it out and anyway when you were close with someone you let them do things for you. We had some variations on this conversation and finally I said, "O.K." It was great! I hadn't realized how much I hated lugging the garbage. It was so great that I not only began letting her take out the garbage, I began counting on it, expecting it, even saving garbage for her. Time passed and then came the familiar feeling of an atmosphere filled with unspoken resentments. So I checked it out. "No, of course she didn't mind." Later when I moved into an apartment with a roommate, my lover mentioned that she was glad I was living with someone since that meant she wouldn't have to take out my garbage.

Recently I was staying at the Pagoda, a lesbian beach resort, and two friends, Beckie and Lynda Lou, had come to visit me for a few days. It was the second day of their visit and the day before we had had a fine time, sharing, having fun, being good friends with each other. I had woken up early and had worked on this paper feeling vulnerable raking over my old journals and excited about the process as well. Later we were getting ready to go out to the beach when my friends went upstairs to the main building (inaccessible to me) to take care of some business. I finished my preparations and went outside and waited at the bottom of the stairs for them to come back down. Beckie appeared and said that mutual friends, Judy and Beth, were making decaf up there in the community kitchen. I made some comment about that we would certainly have to wait for it to be ready (teasing her about her love/addiction to coffee) and then I'm not sure what was said, but somehow it became clear that she was telling me that she was going to spend time visiting with our friends upstairs, that she knew I couldn't get up there, it bothered her that it was inaccessible, but she was going back upstairs. Which she did, leaving me standing at the bottom of the steps... I'd like to tell you that I started screaming my rage up the stairs at her... at the Pagoda for having inaccessible community space, but I didn't. I slunk off to my bedroom and sat on my bed, dry-eyed and staring at the wall.

I could write now about why the more able-bodied lesbian was unable to talk about her resentments and the role of guilt around interactions with disabled people, but I don't want to. I want to write about my feelings and reactions.

What were my options in these first two situations? My immediate solutions were in the one instance to stop drinking coffee and with the other lesbian who I am no longer lovers with, but still have a day-to-day connection, to have never again allowed her to touch my garbage. Even the day we walked into my house and something smelled terribly rotten in it, the fruit flies were swarming, the bag had gotten too heavy for me to lift, and my roommate wasn't home. This is not quite the creative, cooperative style of problem solving I want to believe in.

What if I dramatically say to myself, "I am never going to get in this situation again." What can I do to prevent it? I can interrogate everyone as to their motives before they even lift a sack of my groceries. Or going to the other extreme, I can take people at face value. If they offer to do something for me I'll take them up on it. If they have resentments it's their problem. It's possible for this attitude to work with strangers, but people you are in day-to-day contact with will affect your life with their resentments at some point. As a disabled person, I am very experienced in recognizing resentment as it flits through an emotional atmosphere. So when I choose not to say anything about it I'm setting up an imbalance, a pattern of dishonesty around the issue. In both of these situations I knew what was going on and chose not to confront it until much later. I really liked getting my morning drug and it made my life easier to not have to deal with the garbage, so I ignored the signals I was getting. I had the sense that if I spoke I would risk opening up something too big to handle.

Another option is for me not to hang around lesbians who can't deal with their feelings honestly. I'd be pretty lonely.

And finally I can arrange my life so that many of these issues don't come up. If I have money I can hire someone to take care of a lot of physical chores. If I don't have money then I make choices. I choose not to go out to the movies with friends but stay home and clean up and take out the garbage so that the next day when the lesbian I have this garbage thing with comes over, the issue is not in evidence.

With all these options I realize that I am perpetuating the assumption that figuring all this out is my job and mine alone. What about Beckie and the steps?

After I had been sitting in my bed for a few minutes, Lynda Lou came in and asked if she could help carry my stuff down to the beach. We left walking down the narrow trail, me in front trying not to let her see my tears, pretending to be ok and at the same time thinking that if she just dumped me and my gear on the beach, duty completed, and left to go back up for her stupid coffee, I was going to... scream, die, never speak again, something. When we got to the beach she sat with me, quietly. I was silent, my mind desperately trying to figure out how to be. Eventually I spoke about what had happened in a fairly clinical sort of way. She spoke of having walked out of the bathroom, upstairs, caught the gist of what had happened and had come down to me. She said she wished that I was more of a "fit thrower." Anyway, now I was really scared because my feelings were a little bit out in the open. I no longer had the option of pretending that I hadn't noticed.

A little later Beckie came down to the beach and sat on the

blanket with me. We stared at each other. We stared at the ocean. I was scared. Finally she said, "If you're mad at me why don't you just say so." I blurted out, "I'm angry at you" and we went from there. I can't remember many of our words but she said she knew she really fucked up and she was sorry. I told her how it had felt to me. She didn't know what else she could do, she was sorry, she really fucked up. I cried. She cried. We were winding down, coming to a kind of closure when she said, "You know I love you." I began to sob, and sob, and sob. I felt like it might never stop. I realized how scared I had been to be angry. How necessary Beckie's friendship was in my life. That if I was too much trouble or made her feel bad about herself she might leave me. How scared I had been in other relationships.

With Beckie my solution to the problem was not a clear cut, individual one. It was messy, full of emotion, not really any sort of concrete solution at all, but we did it together and it was and is very satisfying.

What I would like to happen is a realization from an individual or a community that simply because I am in that relationship or part of that community that it is to all our benefits to figure it out together. That has happened in my life, but for the most part it has been up to me to initiate, to solve, and to live with these issues. I desperately want this to change. Giving and receiving help in a way that maintains the respect of both parties, flows back and forth, and enhances intimacy rather than deadens it, has the potential of transforming this production-oriented, work ethic, and individualistic society. I see this as part of my life's work, radical work that will allow me to live a life that is as aware and conscious as possible. It is also work, because of being disabled in this culture, I often have no choice about. It is part of me getting through my daily day.

There are many ways to do this work, but here in this discussion of intimacy, I'd like to begin with myself. I like to think of myself as a politically conscious, working-towards-radical lesbian. I enable, with other lesbians, a feminist bookstore to exist. I'm involved in Lesbian Feminist politics. I'm sometimes outspoken on disability rights. I try to make conscious decisions about how I spend and earn my money, how I relate to others, what food I eat, all as ways of envisioning the type of world I would like to exist and to go ahead and start living that way as much as possible. All this is of course fraught with compromise.

At the same time there are some dubious values that nonetheless operate powerfully in my life. These concepts emerge, in part, from being white and raised vigorously middle class by working class parents in the United States. However, these values become more entrenched in my life because of my experiences as a disabled person, a person traditionally pushed away from paying work and the type of independence it brings. I believe that I must "pull my own weight," "do my share," "never be a burden," and "take care of myself." My self concept is affirmed by earning my own living, running a financially successful business in this economic system, and in general by knowing that I'm a valuable, contributing member of society. Strange beliefs for someone who on another level would like to be actively dangerous to this society. I am afraid to personify any of the stereotypes of disabled people—to be needy or unemployed, to depend on charity, to be childlike, to beg in the streets. These fears block my ability to effect change, to be radical, as well as diminishing my opportunities for having fun.

How would I give and seek help as a radical lesbian, and do it in a way that does not compromise the potential for intimacy? I know that I give help. I also know that I and others act as if it doesn't count as much as the help I get. The world is set up so that an able-bodied person gets through the day with the help of hundreds of devices and services and can still pretend she did it all by herself. I don't get to pretend—this world is set up so that heavy bags of groceries and a long flight of stairs make the need for help glaringly obvious. Even taking this into consideration, I may be simply too exhausted at the end of a day coping with architectural barriers and people's attitudes to "do my share," to keep the give and take "even steven." I'm tired of keeping count. Of not asking one lesbian to help because she already did a "favor" for me today. Of reminding myself I can ask another lesbian because I did her two "favors" last week. I want to know within myself that I am a precious asset to this world and let go of ever needing to prove that to myself or others. If all I was able to do was lie in bed and drool I'd be no less worthy of being loved and cared for with respect.

So often getting help is mixed up with getting love. Our lovers and families are our caretakers. One method for me is to separate help and love. To get help from one place by paying for it, and love and respect and caring from another. It is comfortable for me when I can compartmentalize them in this way and in the world I live in now, it would be an incalculable improvement as well as a viable and healthy option if it were attainable.

Yet I know that this is not the radical solution I ultimately want. That is harder to describe in concrete terms. One way of being radical is to go where your greatest fears are; for me, to embrace some of the disabled stereotypes and allow myself to be needy and childlike. Another way to be radical is to come back full circle to where you started, but on another plane; for me to integrate rather than separate help and love, but in an altered context. This altered context has to do not only with political and economic changes but also with individual and communal transformations on an emotional and spiritual level. This is hard to imagine. It must include a redefinition of how we live in community, some sort of metaphysical belief in being parts of a whole, and a type of free flowing creativity that can lead to practical ideas. This process is not linear. I know that at the same time I am trying to separate help and love in my life, by figuring out which is which I am bringing them together. I know this radical, altered context has existed in my life and I know that the more it happens, even if only for a moment, the more I will begin to recognize it and be able to turn my life in its direction.

Ruth L. Schwartz

The Same Moon

for Pam

1.

Because you danced so sexy, arms above your head,
    and when you saw me watching you,
    you gave me back a smile I could taste,
    and I wanted to swim through the gap between
    your front teeth
    and roll around for hours
    on your warm tongue,

because when I think of you
    my nipples scratch at the front of my shirt
    like chickens wanting to be let out
    into the sweet, wormy grass,

because when we stood talking,
    that first night,
    I saw the moles on your left cheek
    like dark, tiny petals outlined in the bar's
    raw light,

because you woke at 5:00 a.m.,
    needing to go home before
    your children woke,
    and as I drove you on the silent freeway,
    holding your hand in the near-light,
    our breath frosted the windshield on the first day of July,

because I was terrified to call you,
   and called you anyway,
   and loved you anyway,

I thought we might survive it,
the journeying between our different worlds.

2.

After the picnic-blanket day
when we first told our stories,
I knew there was nothing
I could possibly offer you,
   absolutely nothing.
"Except yourself," my roommate said.
"Except yourself," you echoed later.

I grieved your Mississippi childhood,
teachers, white and Black, who didn't want
   to teach Black kids,
the cousin who molested you,
the sister who molested you,
mother gone, father you didn't know.
Thinking the space between your teeth
   was ugly.
Covering your mouth when you smiled.

You brought me flowers, signed the card
"Forever Yours"—words I couldn't understand.
Forever? Mine?

3.

On the road to Monterey
you let me drive the winding parts
played Tracy Chapman on a battered portable
slept against my arm

Your sister's apartment. Her sizing me up—
"She's cute"—as if I wasn't there.
You played with the hair on my leg
while the TV blared
and she talked about the babes she'd fucked.
I felt comfortably ornamental,
nothing at all required of me.

4.

I loved hearing your voice on my answering machine
especially after we started saying
"I love you" to each other
and you'd say it on every message,
sometimes just "'love you,"
leaving the pronoun out
so it became an incantation.

We saw each other so briefly
    between jobs, the kids—

an hour in my too-quiet, booklined room;
when you didn't want to talk,
you'd read the spines aloud,

or an hour at the bar, your world,
you regal as a queen with your Crystal Geyser,

knowing everyone,
leaving every dance, every conversation
   unfinished between us,
introducing me around—
"She's cute," they'd tell you
while I tried to remember names.

5.

Finally I met your children,
bought them Slurpees.
A canyon I'd never seen—
them skipping between, ahead of us
down to the shallow pond where tadpoles swam.
I couldn't believe how easy it was.
I caught some of the little frogs
   with my bare hand
and you chided me like a mother
and they leapt back to their water.

Later, outside my house
with the nightsmelling bush wafting its scent
   to the curb,
I said I loved you
and your whole body seemed to flower
open. You threw back your head.
"Tell me," you said,
and I did, I did.

6.

But you were living in a cheap motel,
   San Pablo Avenue,
you and the kids crammed into one room—

clothes and papers scattered everywhere,
and on one dresser-top, an iron
    held out like a hand,
a lone gesture toward order.

At one end of that motel courtyard
    a tall palm tree waved its fronds—
peaceful, incongruous.
At the other end, a single orange phonebooth,
    a battered phone.
Once when we were talking, you had to get off
because a woman said it was "urgent."
Turned out she was trying
to get some crack.
Turned out she knew you,
had seen you in a meeting once,
back in the hospital, when you were detoxing.
Into the phone she said,
"and give me some extra
for my friend here, too..."
You looked around, wondering who she meant.
Then your palms started sweating
then every part of you started sweating.
"I'm a rock star. I'm famous," she said
(you explained the drug slang to me later.)
"I ain't famous no more," you croaked,
the sweat coating your voice,
dripping through the parking lot,
up the stairs,
back to your one room.

7.

You said you were torn between her and me.
"It's like you each know different parts of me."
We were walking around in your new neighborhood,
but you didn't want to go too far.
"People see a white person,
they'll think you're a cop."
You said the part of you that loved me
was the kid-part, who you were
before the streetlife. Before drugs.
Suddenly I *saw* you,
bright, eager, shining kid.
Beautiful dreamy girl. Shoeless
and alone
down the long, sharply pebbled road.

Where in your life
                    where in mine
could we walk?

8.

Some of the things you said to me:

that   you liked me in tight jeans

that   you weren't right for me
              I should be with a conservative whitegirl
              with a good job

that   you'd always wanted to go to Paris
           be a writer
              help people
              get on a bus and just ride

that   without the kids you'da been
              dead or in jail by now

that   someday I'd thank you
              for keeping me out of your life

that   there was a hummingbird outside,
              drinking the gladioli

that   you'd miss me

              and I said I'd miss what
              happened, and what never did:

              our spirits completely transcending
              and completely barricaded by
              our real lives

9.

Still it goes on opening in me.
Still my breasts like wanting mouths.
Still the grief after I talk to you.
Still the joy, unreasoned.

10.

So few words between us now,
except how we still find each other
    beautiful—

you saying, "turn around,
let me see you in those jeans,"

me with my fingers in your hair,
tight and soft back of your neck,

you warning me it's rough,
it'll cut my hands.

Bonnie Morris

Another Year in the War

In 1981 and 1982 I lived in Israel and studied Jewish law at Tel Aviv University. I shared a dormitory suite with seven other women, all from different countries and with different socioeconomic backgrounds. My own roommate was Brazilian. She spoke Portuguese, Spanish, Hebrew, and English—in that order, and when she felt like it.

Paula was thin, stubborn, and angrily brilliant. She lay face down on her mattress refusing to speak. She brought home large art books from the Tel Aviv University library and copied famous paintings directly from the grand pages, using bits of charcoal, and then threw her very perfect sketches into the garbage can. I would say "I'm going for a walk" and then dash around to the general trash bins behind the dorm to rescue Paula's rumpled-up masterpieces, which I then hid in my desk. Eventually she caught me in the act and never trusted me again. Her most memorable project was a colored clay interpretation of Dante's *Inferno*, with little figurines on shredded newspaper. These tragic statuettes, arranged symbolically across back issues of *Maariv*, sat on our coffee table for months until Paula mashed them in a fit of temper.

At first it seemed we had nothing in common but our Judaism and our revolutionary politics, although these two elements themselves might have given us much to talk about. If Paula was *Sephardi*, I was *Ashkenazi*; if Paula was malcontented and brooding, I was relentlessly cheerful and enthusiastic; she was dark-skinned and I was fair, in a land where this mattered to an alarming degree; no, she did not trust me yet. We were far from our homes and our mothers: that was the first link, the first connecting spark between our careful faces.

Neither Paula nor I had much money. We waited monthly, moodily, for our different scholarship checks. We played cards. She cheated. We groped toward one another in pieces of language, slowly becoming more fluent in each other's idioms. One night I came out to her, and not long after that we reached each other in the easiest language of all.

In the spring of 1982 there was a vacation from university classes, and I decided to go on a camelback trip through the Sinai desert, which was about to become the land of Egypt, according to the Camp David agreements. Paula's government checks had been cut off due to her refusal to enlist in the Israeli Army. The day I left for the Sinai, she left for a *moshav* to work on the banana harvest, where the work was hard and brought a living wage.

At first my trip through the Sinai was a wild thrill. We did ride camels, but mostly hiked on foot, our sturdy boots gently chewing the sandstone canyons and those dried riverbeds called *wadis*. The other kids were mostly American Jewish teenagers and freshmen on semester at the Hebrew University of Jerusalem; we were led by six Bedouin men and one Bedouin woman, Maya. At night we slept on the hard ground, beneath the most astounding panorama of shooting stars I have ever seen. It was entirely like living on another planet. The valleys were filled with fossils and the moans of camels. I forgot academics and learned to bake *pita* on a rock.

On the third or fourth day of the journey, the camel I was riding bolted for no other reason than spite and tried to rub me off on the side of a rocky butte. My left hand was covered with rope burns and scrapes. Maya suggested that I keep my hand warm by sitting near the camp fire that night. Weaving a makeshift bandage from a spare hiking sock, I was absorbed and preoccupied and not quite listening to the chatter of the other

Americans, so I could not tell you when their camaraderie turned into a giggling exchange of racist jokes.

"...and she was some dumb nigger," was the sentence that snapped me to attention. I looked up, startled. These were observant Jewish kids, the boys in *yarmulkes* (which are called *kippot* in Israel) and the girls as well as boys rising each morning to pray. Their concern about anti-Semitism was sincere; most of their families included Holocaust survivors or victims. I was unprepared for their hypocrisy.

I immediately spoke up and asked for an end to the derogatory remarks, as I found them highly offensive—and surprising, from such a group.

There was a profound silence. I had spoken with my eyes downcast, and assumed that upon lifting my gaze from my bandaged wrist I would see a good many shamed and repentant faces. Instead, I was confronted by a ring of hostile eyes and derisive snickers. As I waited, in growing astonishment, for at least one other enlightened soul to come to my aid with a supportive remark about the insidiousness of racism, the group burst into a buzz of angry giggles, and assorted questions were fired at me from the tight circle of young white faces.

"What's the big deal anyway?"

"What's your problem?"

"Why don't you just go back to the 1960's?"

They returned to their blithe talk, their chuckled deprecations of the various black women who had worked as servants for their families back home in New Jersey, in Pennsylvania, in Ohio. Maya stood by impassively, the firelight dancing on her dark skin as she unbraided her hair and carefully drank one swallow of water from her own saddlebag. I stumbled in humiliation to my sleeping bag and wept for Paula, for the future of Israel, for the racism against the Sephardic Jews, against the Arabs, against the women, the women of color in the world. I looked up at the Big Dipper and recalled a day when Paula and I had walked in the park in Ramat Aviv. We sat on a bench by the Yarkon River, enjoying the sunlight. Two young soldiers approached us. They made blatant kissing and sucking noises at me and circled round like sharks, ignoring Paula. One soldier reached for my long blond hair and Paula shouted "Leave her alone" in Hebrew. "Blondini," the soldiers addressed me, "Why are you so beautiful and she so ugly?"

I recalled another day when two young Danish exchange students, classmates of Paula's, came to our dorm room. Paula made them tea, offered chocolate. Finally they stated their business. They needed a part-time maid to clean their apartment. Was Paula interested? (That was the night when Paula smashed her Dante's *Inferno*.)

And I recalled one more incident. I had been on the beach and a tall Sephardic soldier put his hand on me underwater. I angrily splashed the salt Mediterranean in his eyes. He shouted at me "Why won't you let me take you out? Because I am Sephardi! You American women hate us!"—and I had wanted to weep then, too, at the irony, the self-hatred, the distance between us all. And then, as now, I had been too cautious to retort, "Fools! But I live with and love a Sephardi woman."

I must have fallen asleep, for suddenly it was the middle of the night and I needed to urinate. The fire was almost out, the kids and Bedouin guides all snug in their blankets beneath trembling stars. I looked around hopelessly for toilet paper, for I had used the last scrap of mine to clean my bleeding hand that morning. Finally, chagrined, I seized upon a spare sock and walked into the desert. No one seemed awake but the camels, whose teeth-grinding filled the air with eerie bonish moans. I stood unsteadily peeing into the Sinai desert, the land of my ancestors to which I had returned. When I had finished I threw my sock under a tall boulder, behind which, quietly observing my second good cry of the night, Maya sat awake rolling a cigarette.

In the morning no one but Maya would speak to me; the other kids avoided me and made rude remarks behind my back. I compensated by becoming as Bedouin as possible, bartering for desert pants and tribal jewelry from a wizened man who materialized ghost-like from the desert to trade with the guides. As I trudged along in the hot sun, Maya showed me how Bedouin women hammered intricate bracelet designs from the old metal of discarded sardine cans. She showed me how to braid beads into the lock of hair just over my forehead. The other kids snickered as I squatted in the sand with Maya, drawing designs and listening to her stories. "Maya, woman of the desert," someone said disparagingly.

I had had enough. When we reached the first road we had seen in five days, I decided to leave the tour, having exhausted my reserve of group cooperativeness. I gathered my belongings from the camel's back, gave Maya my remaining citrus fruits, and bade her *salaam alechem*. Then I jumped on the first bus I could flag down. It was a tourist bus crammed with aging Scandinavians, who, despite my desert clothes, took one look at my blond hair and began to make unkind remarks to me in Danish about the Arabs.

It was Friday, the Sabbath approaching within a few hours. There would be one last bus leaving Eilat for Jerusalem before all buses stopped running until Saturday night. I purchased a ticket and slept on the bus, rousing myself only to eat two rolls and a sack of mocha-milk at a desert kibbutz station.

In Jerusalem there was noise. And quiet. Then noise again as the Arab shopkeepers opened their stalls on Saturday morning for business. I had many hours to kill until the buses began running again, and sat in a youth hostel drinking tea with milk and banana powder, aching to be in Tel Aviv, to be with Paula, to cleanse myself of the past few days. There was no working shower at my youth hostel; I lay in bed to spare my aching and blistered feet, still wrapped in the seven pairs of socks I had needed to cushion myself against the rocky Sinai pathways. Down the hall from me a woman played the radio, relentlessly changing the dial between the Voice of Peace and *Reshet Gimel*, and suddenly one of Paula's favorite songs drifted in to me. I squeezed my pillow in anguish, wanting her, afraid to tell her all I had seen and heard in the desert. When I could stand it no longer, I hoisted pack on back and walked to the bus stop at Jaffa Gate to sit stubbornly upon a hard bench.

A Hasidic man, wearing the customary black suit, hat, ritual fringes and earlocks of the ultra-Orthodox Jews, paused as he passed by me, then said in Hebrew, "You know today is Shabbos, and no bus until six?"

"I know," I replied in English, my mind on Paula's artistic rendition of Dante's *Inferno*.

His expression changed. "You are American? You are Jewish?"

"Yes," I said.

"Would you care to learn for a moment with me about the Torah?" he invited, gesturing to a park across the road where there were benches shielded from the sun. I was surprised—most Hasidic men avoid women and will not address them in public—but I was also curious. I wanted a chance to learn more about Hasidism, and was pleased to have the opportunity to question this gentleman about his beliefs. Feeling better, I followed the Hasid into the park.

We walked for quite a ways and then settled ourselves on a secluded bench. "Do you speak Yiddish?" he enquired. "My

English is poor."

"No, all I know are insults and affectionate slang."

"Ha! Ha!" he roared, throwing what I assumed was a fatherly arm around me. "You are wonderful. We are all one family, Jews, yes?" And before I knew what to say he had kissed me plumply on the mouth.

I was so incredulous that I could only laugh in his face. Of course I knew that no male Hasid ever touches any woman except for his mother, his wife, or his daughters. He will not sit beside a strange woman on a bus, nor take change directly from a woman's hand in a shop. I had heard, in Israel, about a few repressed Hasidim who turned to molesting American girls, but it seemed ludicrous that I'd attracted one in my present state.

He was singing, or chanting, in Yiddish, and offered me an apple. I had the feeling he wasn't particularly bright. I sighed and said "Look, I'd better go," knowing my bus wasn't due for at least two more hours.

"Sit down," he intoned with jovial deadliness. "Do I not make you feel good?" He pinned me to the bench, pressing a hand to my breasts and trying to force pieces of apple into my mouth. Inexpertly, he kissed me again. As he relaxed his stranglehold, I grabbed my knapsack and raced down the path, preparing to scream if he followed.

He did not. Forlorn, stupid, he called nervously after me, "When can I see you again? Will you come back to Jerusalem?"

Yes, I would come back to Jerusalem, City of Peace, as the Jews had returned to the Sinai, where they had once awaited the revelation of the Ten Commandments. There was no peace in 1982, and the Sinai I had wandered in echoed with the sound of broken commandments. Was there room for women, for dark-skinned women, for women who loved women, in this land? Did Paula and I exist as Jews?

"AaaH!" roared Paula when I limped into our dorm suite at last. *"Minha bambina! Que fofina!* Baby! Well, I'm okay now." She was covered with cuts and scabs from a week of banana harvests. She had ended her work hiatus with a trip to an archaeological dig and announced, as I soaked my feet in a bucket of hot water, "I have ten thousand years of history in my hair."

Together we cleaned our wounds and then took supper into our room: black bread and rice, avocado and cheese, white chocolate and some of Paula's excellent Brazilian coffee. In between mouthfuls, I spoke of my experiences in the Sinai, in Jerusalem.

"I wish you drank coffee in the mornings so I could bring it to you in bed," was all Paula had to say.

"Ma la asot," I complained. "I've run the gamut of religious perversions."

"They all crazy," said Paula.

"I can't believe I let him touch me," I said, shaking.

"Tell him to fuck off!" Paula growled. "You are mine, mine, mine. *Eo mujer macho.* So they call me in Brasil."

I went into the tiny bathroom we shared with six other women and showered, showered, rivers of desert grit streaming off my tired legs. Then I threw my towel over the door and walked naked to bed.

"You need a little action," said Paula.

"I think I've had plenty today already."

"Not Latina," she reminded me.

Eventually it was 11:49 p.m., or, as the Israeli-made clock showed it, 23:49. "This is proof that I cannot be a tourist," I spoke into the creamy underside of Paula's breast. "I attempted the tourist basics: to ride a camel, sit around a campfire with other young Jewish students, talk theology with a Hasidic rabbi. I failed at all three, my purpose and perspective so utterly attached to our life here in this hot, cramped, cockroach-ridden room. Perfect happiness. You are the miracle I saw in the desert. No one saw it but me."

"*Maspik*," said Paula. "I make some good for you, you make some good for me."

"They were right. Israel is dangerous."

"And you, bambina? Your hands are Bedouins tonight. Always wandering."

The television screen showed tanks full of Israeli soldiers rolling into Lebanon while women in both countries wailed inconsolably.

I wrapped myself around Paula's brown limbs. "This is the only safety, the only peace."

Paula laughed a little in the dark. "You gonna remember me."

****

Maariv: a popular Israeli newspaper.

Sephardi, Ashkenazi: Sephardic Jews are descended from and
follow the rituals of those Jewish communities in
Spain, Portugal, Turkey, Italy, and other Mediterranean countries. Ashkenazic Jews are generally
considered to encompass Jews descended from
Slavic and Northern European countries. In Israel,
political and social conflict has risen from the sec-
ond-class status often ascribed to Sephardic Jews;

until recently the Ashkenazic Jews controlled Parliament and most positions of power. There are obvious racial and ethnic connotations to this dilemma.

Moshav: a collective farm, but with private ownership (unlike a *kibbutz*).

Wadi: Arabic term for dried riverbed path cutting a way through the desert.

Pita: flat bread.

Yarmulke, kippot: small knitted skullcaps worn by Orthodox Jewish males.

Salaam alechem: Arabic greeting or farewell, "Peace be with you."

Reshet Gimel: an Israel radio station (Gimel is G in the Hebrew alphabet).

Minha bambina, que fofina: Brazilian terms of endearment: "My baby, so cute."

Ma la asot: Hebrew for "What can you do?" (spoken resignedly).

Eo mujer macho: Portuguese for "I am a masculine woman."

Maspik: Hebrew for "Enough."

Paula Amann

Cookery

My love she speaks in parsley
in garlic and well-simmered marinara
in Mediterranean olive flesh
dark and tangy as freckles.
Goat cheese may crumble unto crackers
as we sip our wine by the sea
but her pie crust will endure
three cross-country flights as she does
smiling and be pressed into service
with blueberry and custard core.

She's not easy on the telephone
but look how the rounds of pink trout
drown in herbal cream sauce and
succulent chunks of red pepper
and just as in the fairy tales
the table is suddenly groaning
with cheesy au gratin potatoes
coriander-flecked carrots and
the challah lies plump and shining
under the double flames.

She could care less where things lie
on the staircase in the cellar
but see how the pita bread wedges
make planetary rings around the platter
and a blaze of paprika marks the center
where baba ghanoush and hummus meet
as thick as spiced as the accent from Haifa

as the cookery of a summer night when
mingling sauces and other ingredients
we bring each other slowly to a boil.

Subtleties

It's not only landscapes
mapped on each other's bodies
with fingertips and tongues
but the way you make two coffees,
lather all the dishes
while I pour cherry juice
and toast banana muffins
the morning after.

It's not only the vase
of storm-blue irises
you brought with rueful eyes
a week after words,
but puff pastry and Chardonnay
you pull from your overnight bag
like a magician.

It's not only phone calls
dialed as promised,
but the night when the bomb
fell near your sister's house,
the day your cancer test
came out clean.

It's not just the aerogram
you scribbled from Jerusalem
full of ancient streets
and current longings,
but the messages encoded
in a stroke
of your freckled hand.

Cristina Salat

Who Will Lead?

"Will you go to my prom with me?" my new friend Gina asks one Saturday as we sit on the beach.

I turn my face from the ocean to look at her, in shock.

"I've thought about this a lot," she continues, busily molding a shape in dry sand. "And I want to take someone I feel comfortable with. And since we've talked about stuff like this..." her voice dwindles off as her eyes dart sideways, checking me out.

"Oh boy," I say.

Yes, we have talked about stuff like this—as research for my children's books. She is the most articulate of those who responded to my ad: LOOKING FOR TEENAGERS TO INTERVIEW, and we're becoming pals.

"So, will you go? It's June 14th, at the Hilton."

I believe in this. What else can I say, but yes?

"Great!" Gina turns her body to face me, all smiles now. "I thought we could both go femmy." She pulls her long black ponytail forward to chew on thoughtfully, ready to plan details. "What do you think?"

"Sure," I say, though I haven't worn a dress since leaving Manhattan's corporate world. Still, I have nothing against dresses, and really, this could be a prime research experience. I'll make a short story out of it, and call it *Senior Ball* or *Prom Night*. It'll be like a modern day fairy tale, or maybe a young Harlequin romance. I haven't written anything light in quite a while.

"There's one thing I should tell you," Gina says, looking out to sea again. "Everybody else will be going boy-girl... and I'm not the most popular person at school."

"No problem," I say, planning the story. So what if 28 is somewhat old to be anyone's prom date?

In the coming weeks, I casually mention the high school dance to my friends.

"Let me get this straight. You're going to a prom, at a white bread school, in Los Gatos?" Nwanda asks in disbelief.

"A baby dyke," my roommate Sharon laughs. "You lucky dog! Are you going to spend the night together at the hotel?"

My friend Marcus frowns. "Isn't that dangerous?" he asks. He has not been carefree since the incident outside Boy Club, so I quickly reassure him.

"It's an organized event. There'll be teachers."

"What about afterwards?"

The next time Gina phones, I question her.

"How do you think the other students will react to us going together?"

She is silent for a minute. "They won't like it."

Her quietness sinks to the bottom of my stomach. Visions of tuxedoed football players surrounding the two of us in a deserted parking lot fill my mind. I reach quickly for another image.

"What kind of corsage would you like?"

On Friday night, June 13, I burrow into the back of my closet and remove armloads of plastic-wrapped dresses. I snap a classical tape into my bedroom stereo, and then change my mind and replace it with The Sundays, something new, to get me in the right mood. Wispy voices and synthetic music fill the room. I hop around a bit in front of the full-length mirror, mimicking steps from MTV.

In search of the perfect prom dress, I try on every one I own. The purple paisley is too office-like; the yellow cotton, not festive enough; and the black cocktail dress with its lowcut back—sexy. Much too sexy.

I laugh at my reflection in the mirror. What I need is a chameleon dress. One that will change, depending on who's looking.

I want to look good. Appropriate for the photographs Gina will put into her scrapbook. Her hot date with an older woman when she was 17.

But I also want to wear something that will cover up as much of me as possible, yet be loose enough to fight in, should I need to. Something that will make me appear respectable, maybe even matronly, to the dance chaperones. I don't want them wondering if I will be robbing the cradle that night.

An anxious face gazes back at me from the mirror. I try to relax the worry wrinkling my forehead. This is supposed to be fun, I remind myself. Research.

Saturday I do not eat all day. I don't do any writing, talk on the phone or clean my house. I spend the day on my couch, stroking the cat and looking through photo albums of me when I was 17. Would I have been brave enough to take a woman to my prom? Would Gina be doing this now if she didn't have adults—like me—touting the importance of people being themselves?

Am I being myself, wanting to seem asexual so I won't offend anyone... or turn anyone on?

When Gina picks me up that night, I am wearing the fitted black dress with a string of pearls. My back feels conspicuously naked, but I ignore it.

"Tweet twoo," Gina whistles.

"You too," I smile.

Embarrassed, she adjusts the large copper earrings that match her dress. Her hair is fresh-washed and blow-dried into a breezy sculpture. Bronze powder lightly dusts her cheeks. I notice her knees. Peeking out from the shiny outfit, they seem incredibly small.

We exchange corsages and Sharon takes many pictures of us against the hallway wall. Then a rented limousine glides us away.

Our driver doubleparks in front of a grand gold and white Hilton.

"Are you ready?" Gina whispers, clutching my arm. I nod, and we get out.

As we walk into the hotel, side by side, we are surrounded by dapper young men and sleek young women. My high-heeled feet don't feel the carpeted floor. We swim through a sea of white faces, and I feel very brown. My eyes are unfocussed, but my skin is aware of the heads that turn to stare at us.

"Mr. Gaberdine, this is Cristina Salat," Gina says to her principal at the check-in table.

"Pleased to meet you," the stout, bald man booms, shaking my hand vigorously. He pretends not to notice that I am not a boy, or even a teenager.

We walk inside the ballroom, another sea of white—white balloons, linen-covered tables, and a mirrored globe revolving snow light everywhere.

On the table nearest us, a girl in green chiffon pushes away her plate of chicken.

"Oh God, I've lost my appetite," she says loudly.

Next to me, Gina shrinks, pulling her heart inward. I look over at her and she looks back.

"This is ridiculous," I say. She nods, wanting to believe me. "Are *you* hungry?" I ask, loud enough for everyone around us to hear. "I'm starving. I haven't eaten a thing all day."

"Me too," she says, following my lead. Courageously, she reaches for my right hand, which is shaking.

"Hey, Gina!" someone calls from a few tables away. "Over here."

She recognizes the voice. "Those are my friends," she tells me, tugging on my fingers.

She steps forward, and this time I follow.

Sue Russell

But Is She Jewish?

My lover practices Yiddish for the sounds,
for the pucker of schmaltz and schmooze
and two fingers over the throat
to test the deepening guttural.
Yes, I say, you're getting close.
That's almost it.
Two women on the fringed settee
and somehow it feels like home.
Boxes upon boxes. My books and
her books, her small breasts.
Marking the days with my hands.

Diana Aleyn Cohen

Cancer Poem

What am I to do with this
This notion that you have cancer
I was just getting used to
The oversized heart
Beating beneath your soft smooth chest
Against my cheek
Its erratic dance
The bottles of pills

I was just rejoicing after the doctor's
Last report   the x-rays showing
An almost normal muscle
Your body responding
To the meds
The day of our loving
Stretching out to the
Razor thin horizon

What am I to do with this
This notion that you never broke
Your back in some
Ski accident but had
Pieces of toxic spine removed and
Others weakened by radiation
Hair falling out in clumps around your
Sixth grader's white and graceful
Neck

Already I have pictured your parents
Signing the forms
The administration of that
Hopeful chemical which
Did its job and
Took one quarter of your heart
As pay

I have already been cautious
Of the steel rods
Running the length
Of your back
Leg bone and rib
Grafted with metal
Into structure
Bracing sternum through to spine
Preventing collapse
A different kind of skeleton
Man-made, skyscraping
Holds you up

I have listened to you
Touching firmly
Or not at all
Have been afraid
The rods would
Come poking through
Been reassured when I read
The thickest skin of the body
Covers the back
The orthopoedist saying
To your shoulder pains
Most people with these rods

Don't live this long

I have touched the scars
A map of surgeries and
Kissed the tiny hairless spots
At your temples where
They drilled holes in your skull
In the name of healing
Ran pegs through your knees
And called it halo
Traction

I have pictured your body
Strapped to long boards
You are being turned quickly
Open-mouthed
Motionless in a moving frame
A sore throat afterwards your
Only reminder of screaming
I have tried to see
What you took in
Through your wide blue eyes
Royal sky after sunset
Looking out at hospital
Hospital hospital
For months on end
Tile floor green wall
White ceiling

Your parents
Throwing Christmas in July
For you
Would be dead by December

Fourteen years later
You are still here
The sweetest touch
I've ever known
And what am I
To do

I have tried to feel my hands
Moving me along parallel bars
Learning to walk
My muscles
Learning to pee
To push and contract
Hours for a drop
My young body
Thin and fragile
Opened over and over
Incision

But I cannot
Ever
Know what you went through
It is so far from me
An astronaut's trip to the moon
A cat's dream
The colored scales of fish

But now at least your scattered puzzle stories
Form a perfect tale
The jagged final piece
That you have cancer

And when you tell me first
I say
That's scary
  (I want you to tell me
  When you will die
  Why can't you tell me
  When you will die
  Does outliving the predictions mean
  No time or
  Plenty of it
  I want to scream and rattle bars
  For now I'm sure that
  You will die
  Much too soon
  I am trying to feel me
  I am trying to feel you
  I am trying
  Not to feel)

We wager on what will kill you
Muscle or bone
I joke that it could be a bus
You say you're sure it will be
Peaceful

I am very good at
Knowing news is true
While feeling it's a lie
Pretending to be
Dreaming

I ask you how it feels
To be inside your body

You say it's all become a part
Your body is all one
But you don't know
How the person that is you
Got inside that body

I wonder
Should I change
Must I revise
My pictures of you
I do not want to see
Every cell of bone
An alien invader
Toxic
Danger
Enemy within
Bone is too much of you
To hate
To fear

I want to love your body
As before
Fiercely
Tenderly
As one
To let in all that's true

I don't know what to do
With this fourteen year remission
Loving you and waiting
I need to learn to love you
Without waiting.

Amy Edgington

If

If I wear jeans and a tie
You will not know who I am.
If I put on a long black dress and beads
You will not recognize me.
There is nothing in this world
I can wear that would not be a disguise;
And even these costumes do not fit my body
Because I'm not only queer, I'm bent.
If I take off all my clothes
You might see less of who I really am.
Even if you closed your eyes
you might only touch curves and angles
where you did not expect to find them.
And if I knew how to remove
This disguise of flesh and bone
And show you my naked mind and spirit,
Would you turn away from my madness?
And if you could learn to recognize me all ways—
Dressed and undressed, mind and soul and body—
Would you be able to bear my beauty?
Would you be brave enough to love me?

Strip Tease

This poem
is all I have on.
It cannot hide
the way my spine curves
like a swan's neck
or my growing carapace.
One shoulder will ride higher, one hip will march ahead,
while my ribs protrude like mismatched wings.

These are some of the ways I am not like you.
Face it: I am not like you.
Take off your pretense
and stare or blush or giggle.
I'd rather meet you naked
than covered with smiles
that make me
disappear.

Impatient Womanifesto

I am called a hunchback,
and this is an honorable title.
Do not bother with such kind and impartial words
as deformed, disfigured or disabled.
I am not a disease: you
are the ones with dis-ease

and you definitely are not normal.
During most of our history you would have revered me
as a healer and a prophet; you would have believed
that to touch me would bring you
prosperity and fortune. Today you invoke
the psychic powers of hunchbacks,
saying, "I have a hunch,"
even though you may now
shun those of us who do.
Yet you do not believe you are
superstitious, abnormal or cruel.

The churchmen did not think they were superstitious
when they burned us as witches.
The Nazis did not believe they were abnormal
when they gassed us to perfect their methods.
The doctors do not think they are cruel
when they prescribe surgery
to make one leg shorter or longer,
steel rods in the spine, steel pins
in the skull for traction, braces
for the duration of adolescence—
all so we will not become too ugly to get married.
(Touching us has certainly brought the doctors
prosperity and fortune.)

But now I am im-patient:
impatient with painful, cosmetic treatments;
impatient with stares and invisibility;
impatient with pity and insults.
I am impatient when a drunk Lesbian tells me
to stand up straight and be proud.
I am impatient when a sober Lesbian tells me
she can cure me in six weeks with acupuncture.

Listen to me Sisters, if you're not
superstitious, abnormal or cruel:
Why would I want to be straight?
I am bent and proud and beautiful.
Touch me and let me touch you.
Maybe I could tell your future.
Maybe I could cure what ails you.

Joanna Kadi

Love, Space Aliens, and Politics

In a moment forever etched in my mind, *The Weekly World News* alerted my lover and me to our different class locations. As I drove, Jan read various articles aloud, including one about a spaceship and its inhabitants crashing through the roof of a suburban home. It startled a 12-year-old boy sitting in his bedroom watching television.

"Well, I don't know if space aliens really went into his bedroom," I said. "But I know one thing for sure."

"What?"

"That is one rich kid. Any kid with a TV in his bedroom is rich."

Jan gave me a strange look. "I had a TV in my bedroom."

I'm grateful to the *WWN* for its help in pinpointing a key issue in our relationship. In retrospect, I'm angered that political awareness hadn't done it. But from several years of organizing within the left to my more recent foray into lesbian feminist politics, I'd never taken part in a discussion about my class location. I had a great analysis of racism and classism as it applied to the Two-Thirds World[1] and of sexism in my life and the lives of other women. But my own race and class? Obviously unimportant, at least to the white, middle-class people defining movement parameters.

I brought that lack of awareness to my lesbian relationship, although thankfully we read the *WWN* article during our first

---

[1] I use the term Two-Thirds World instead of the racist, hierarchical term 'Third World.'

year together. We've come a long way in the last five years learning how an Arab-Canadian, working-class, able-bodied lesbian and a white, upper middle-class, able-bodied lesbian can be in a relationship.

I believe there are two key items essential for a lesbian couple attempting to deal in just and appropriate ways with race and class differences. First is reassessing our ideas about intimate relationships and love; second is being aware of interrelationship dynamics and taking action.

In this essay I will focus on classism because of time and space constraints and because racism is not as much of a struggle for us. One reason for this is lesbian feminists as a group have done more work on race than on class. Although we still have a long way to go, resources on racism are available for anyone who wants them. Not so with classism. I'm waiting for the anthologies, the speak-outs, and the day when I hear "We need a working-poor/working-class person" when we're choosing categories of speakers for events.

Love and Intimate Relationships

Like everything else in society, love is political because it involves power. It's a mistake for lesbians to ignore that fact and fall into the kind of thinking that defines lesbian love as warm, gushy feelings. Why? Because power inequalities between women are rampant. No matter how much we care about a lover, we cannot magically transcend social structures such as racism that have existed for centuries and been inculcated into each of us since birth. Ignoring these political realities means oppression will be an ongoing reality between lovers. Without hard work, no white woman can engage in a relationship with a woman of colour without perpetuating racism. For example, the white woman may sexually exploit the woman of colour through eroticizing her as "Other" or choose to remain ignorant of her lover's cultural heritage.

Some white lesbians offer the "I love you for yourself. It doesn't matter to me if you're a woman of colour" perspective. This trivializes racism, and offers a limited and liberal perspective on our differences. It also stops us from asking critical questions about who we are attracted to, and why. Why are some white women always attracted to women of colour? Why are some wealthy women always attracted to women from lower classes? Power imbalances are constructed as sexually exciting in this society, and lesbians aren't immune to acting out these scenarios.[2]

We empower ourselves when we define the institutions of love and sexual attraction, not only socially but personally. Scrutinizing our intimate relationships from many angles— emotional, sexual, political, psychological—allows for clarity and perceptive analyses. Examining a relationship politically involves asking questions: What are our respective social locations? How can we deal in healthy, just ways with power differences? What does it mean to love an oppressed person?

To some degree, lesbian feminists as a group understand that love and intimate relationships need critical examination. That's a key belief underlying our work around marital rape, wife battering, child sexual abuse, date rape. We've also critiqued the sexist underpinnings of heterosexual romantic love.

But that work came from an analysis of power differences based on sexism, and I don't believe we've pushed beyond that. We've rejected the dominant culture's notion that heterosexual love is above definition, analysis, and critical questioning but stopped short of examining lesbian love. I believe this is partly, perhaps mostly, because many of us have clung to the simplistic

---

[2] In discussing the need for critical examination, I am not advocating a position whereby love/sexual attraction is nothing more than a social construction that needs to be done away with.

analysis offered by lesbian feminists in the 1970s and 1980s—that sexism is the dominant oppression, and thus relationships between two women are inherently equal by virtue of both being female.

Our community resources reflect this. Finding resources for couples with sexual problems stemming from one or both partners surviving child sexual abuse is easy. Finding resources for couples experiencing problems stemming from one person's ableism is next to impossible. I believe this happens because child sexual abuse can be explained with our single-issue analysis of sexism while ableism cannot. Neither can lesbian battering. It's been said by almost every battered lesbian who has sought support: our communities don't know how to deal with the issue because we don't want to acknowledge it exists. But then lesbian battering doesn't fit with an analysis of the inherent equality of lesbian relationships.

The one thing battered lesbians have is a term to describe their experiences. What about a couple experiencing confusion and inexplicable rupture in their relationship because of class difference? What about a working-class lesbian feeling crazy and stupid, unable to pinpoint and identify the oppression inherent in her middle-class lover's assumptions, ideas, and ways of living?

Little is available for that woman, outside of personal resources and knowledge. The one action she and her lover may take is going to therapy. While ideally therapy offers couples a chance to communicate better and process through difficult issues, its aim is not discerning and articulating political differences. It's highly unlikely any lesbian-feminist therapist would pick up class dynamics.

I've been in short-term therapy with Jan where we learned helpful communication skills, but my gratitude doesn't change my wariness and skepticism. Therapy does not concern itself with power differences between lesbians. How many lesbian-feminist therapists have integrated analyses of racism, classism, sexism, heterosexism, ableism, ageism, and fat oppression? How many can help couples identify these issues and the ways they are manifested in the relationship? None that I've seen. Therapy personalizes relationships, rather than analyzing them structurally and politically. Even if interpersonal dynamics between the lovers offer clues about power differences, therapists miss the signals. Two lesbians being wrenched apart by classism won't get help figuring that out in therapy. If anything, the middle-class biases of therapy will favour the middle-class lesbian and further silence the working-class or working-poor lesbian.

Awareness and Action

The second point I want to explore is the political awareness and action necessary between lovers. Without words and concepts to describe our political/social identities, experiences and reactions, we can't explain ourselves to each other. Yet many lesbian feminists are only aware of social location as it relates to sex and sexual orientation, ignoring equally important locations of race, class, ability, size and age. It's vital we not continue the silence around these issues, either in political communities or intimate relationships.

Most lesbian feminists know how to analyze oppression. We have incredibly sophisticated understandings of sexism and heterosexism, gleaned from discussing, reading, listening, thinking, and acting. And although this seems to be a hard concept for some lesbians to grasp, the same format works for every other oppression.

Jan and I needed to discuss, read, listen, think and act about classism, once *The Weekly World News* and space aliens helped us understand our different class locations. One place class tensions ran high was at Jan's parents' house. During each visit, I experienced constant class attacks[3], felt uneasy and anxious, and would return home physically ill. Every time we sat down to that groaning table with fine china, real silver, and linen napkins, I panicked and prayed I wouldn't break or spill anything. A particularly clear example occurred when we visited Omaha for the funeral of Jan's mother. Within a day, I realized that although I had brought my best outfit to wear to church, her family would be insulted if I showed up wearing it. After an intense period of depression (i.e., anger and shame turned inward), I figured out what was happening. Jan's emotional support and reassurance were not enough, so we visited the mall and used a credit card to buy clothes we couldn't afford.

Suppose Jan and I had gone to a therapist with these concerns, before we realized what was happening. Would a therapist have asked about, and explained, class differences? Would that even have crossed her mind? She might suspect homophobia, and ask whether the family treated me decently. I would say for the most part, they do. Then the problem would become mine. Perhaps my self-esteem is too low, although the political reasons for this would not be discussed. Perhaps I have so much internalized homophobia I am projecting it onto them. Perhaps if Jan and I communicated more effectively, it wouldn't happen. It's true that better communication helped us, but only when coupled with political knowledge and a power analysis. The only political issues therapists have previously brought to such discussions are sexism and heterosexism, in effect, mirroring back the analyses most lesbian feminists have a handle on.

Therapy would not have taken Jan and me to a place of keen awareness around class that includes a power analysis. And

---

[3] Four women, all of us working-class and in a graduate program together, used this term to refer to feelings of panic, insecurity, self-hatred, powerlessness and confusion that resulted from experiencing some aspect of class oppression in a particularly vivid way.

when I say awareness, I don't mean the kind of awareness so popular these days—honouring our differences. What this usually means is articulating differences ("You're Native. I'm white.") then proceeding with business as usual and following a white middle-class agenda. It's the liberal ideology at work once again. Let's celebrate diversity without a political analysis. Let's honour differences as long as we don't take power seriously.

A political analysis of power is crucial for any lesbian couple dealing with issues of race and class. It's not enough for Jan and me to know that she's white and middle-class and I'm a working-class person of colour; we need to understand how that translates into power. Because she has more of it than I do. She comes from a whole line of people who move with authority and confidence in the world. My experience is quite the opposite. Her familiarity with power around race and class identity carries over into our relationship while my familiarity with its lack also carries over.

For us to examine these issues with a liberal analysis of "honouring our differences" would be a travesty. Nothing would change. We must move beyond that liberal analysis and understand who has power, how it's being used, and how to change the dynamics. And it's folly to think the problem can be solved by Jan giving up her power. The notion of a privileged group using downward mobility as a response to power differences is a cowardly way of avoiding responsibility. It's not what oppressed groups want, and it's an unworkable strategy for changing the world.

Awareness and action overlap. Both are necessary when learning about power dynamics and making changes in the relationship. Political action in the larger community and society is, I believe, key for strengthening a relationship and implementing new ideas within it. Jan and I had been activists before we became involved, and our continued activism helped us in regard to issues of race and class, particularly as we began choosing our involvement in political groups based on whether those issues were addressed. We sought out friends and political allies who are working-class and/or of colour. For example, when we lived in Boston with its large, politically-active Arab community, we chose to attend events in that community focussed around the liberation of Palestine, instead of events with white, middle-class gay/lesbian leadership and participants.

What happened once we understood class differences seriously? First of all, a major source of confusion was cleared up. I stopped feeling crazy, stupid, and/or ashamed. Class became a regularly-talked-about subject, not simply when problems arose, but in our day-to-day lives. Our relationship strengthened, partly as a result of the attitudes we brought to the issue. Jan took me seriously enough to do the work involved, and I believed in her enough to expect she would act appropriately and ethically, as opposed to using guilt or shame as a motivating tactic. Our political work is more powerful. Recently, at a workers' benefit at a local union hall, I looked around at the working-class, multiracial audience and felt like I had come home.

Summary

What about lesbian feminist politics? After leaving a six-year marriage to come out, I believed the rhetoric that "Sisterhood is beautiful." It's a tad embarrassing to admit now, but I honestly expected lesbian lovers would be equals because of our femaleness. After six years of being stomped on by a man, I was more than ready for relationships where power differences based on sexism weren't the norm.

I'm not berating anyone for analysis derived years ago in the first blush of lesbian feminism when we really thought women were equals. Today I find it unbelievable so many of us still believe sexism is the real problem, and refuse to move to an integrated analysis of race, sex, class, sexual orientation, size, ability and age. How can anyone still believe a relationship between two women is devoid of power imbalances? Or that the only power differences in heterosexual relationships are based on sex? Although it took time for me to realize, I now know racism and classism were as much at work in the abuse perpetrated by my white, middle-class ex-husband as sexism. An integrated analysis of various forms of oppression is as necessary in our intimate relationships as it is in our political work.

I've focussed here on lesbian relationships, although it's clear these ideas apply to friendships, political organizations, and gay, bisexual or heterosexual relationships. But I do have a special interest in lesbian relationships, since we have so few resources to help us through this uncharted territory. Most resources to date focus on lesbian sex, which is necessary and helpful but not enough. I want subsequent generations of lesbian couples to have tangible resources to help them deal with social and political differences, and to have paradigms of just, healthy relationships across social locations. My hope is that lesbians will read *The Weekly World News* only for news, entertainment and gossip, and that our own communities will alert us to important relational dynamics.

Berta Freistadt

To a Young Woman

Listen I am old sister child
I remember Suez my first glimpse of mortality
The man on the corner would call out death
Before we all had television and could turn off
I saw my own face in the mirror of his breath

Before you shouted your first protest
Stretched your first lung before you
Taught yourself to withdraw
I was wandering in a wilderness too cold for locust
Or honey I too was looking for translation
Looking to learn the local tongue

When you were inside her arms
Sucking at your first mother's breast
I had bought a ticket North my own iron
And fled the pelican nest there I learnt to kiss
Upsidedown to wear lampshades on my head
There I slept on floorboards in a forest I
Climbed a hill of cars and learnt by letter
About death

While you counted building bricks and clattered
In short socks feeding ducks and pigeons in the park
I have wept before redheaded children who smiled
And broke me I have danced for praise and money
Into the empty eyeful dark

Listen I am old sister child
My grey hair was earnt
My torn eyes have seen me crack mirrors
My tired mouth sucked these fingers when they burnt
I remember long empty years when I reproduced
Myself time after time after time I circled dizzy
With the dust that fluffed my fears

I remember my shrinking heart now obstinate
And falter where did I learn to beat it strong
My hand was always full of warning though
Someone whispered once the line of life was long
I knew the pictures and the numbers never matched
It was a thing I couldn't alter

Only in aeroplanes when I looked down on clouds
And glaciers could I forget how much I'd cried
Only with wrists in running water cold as ice
Could I forget the frozen years I sometimes died

I am old sister child
Each day was hacked in me
Scratched in me with a penknife dipped in brine
I cried on my birthday
I doubted my mother
I avoided my father's eyes
I betrayed friends
I stole got lost I told my lover lies
I died many little deaths

All this takes time

Debby Earthdaughter

House Dinner

With only one it's not so bad. I can often think and even speak. With three of them, and one of me, it's hard. At these "house dinners," cozy feature of cooperative living in a groovy feminist house, sometimes I feel like *I'm* being cooked!

Tonight Judy's talking about the neighbors downstairs. She saw a broken safe in the common basement! She's sure they're thieves now.

My mind swirls. I get up and say I'm making tea, does anybody want any?

In the kitchen, I still hear their voices, all agreeing in disgust. But I have some room to think.

When they talk about the neighbors it's always this way. "They don't have steady jobs, they drink too much, they're so loud. They may be criminals." They draw a line. A thick line between themselves and *them*. But where do I fit on that line, straddling it? It's unclear.

How do I say to them that the mother reminds me of my mom when she was younger? Even though I got a headache from the cigarette smoke, it felt like home to me to be briefly in their kitchen, with the cracked table, her smoking and laughing, her best friend giving her a haircut.

How do I say that I have stolen too, will again if hungry or without something I need? That because Judy and I are able to get OK jobs and Lisa and Kelly get family help to go to grad school doesn't mean everyone can? We have a lot more privilege. If my only job choice was to work in fast food for minimum wage year after year, I'd probably opt for thieving too.

It doesn't mean I love the neighbors. I do suspect that the oldest son broke into our place. I didn't have anything stolen—

no portable valuables. But it was still a violation. My housemates lost cameras, expensive tape players, jewelry. They lost more, and also had more to lose and more ability to replace things.

The oldest son and maybe the mother are beating the younger kids. I called Child Protective Services because I wish someone had intervened when I was a kid. But I know the classism of it too. Middle class social workers come out. They or their friends could be beating their own kids, but who will hear in their suburban homes?

Well, the water's boiling. Pour the tea. I'll let it steep in here along with my thoughts.

When it is just one of the two who are my friends, Judy and Lisa, who I feel love for, who have been overall good in my life, I can often speak.

When Lisa said how most people are stupid, I was thrown for a minute. But came back in and said how that was classist. Most people haven't had her educational opportunities.

When Judy talked about summer camp like it was a universal experience, I said how camp was a middle class thing that most kids didn't get to go to.

With the wealthiest one, Kelly, it is real hard. She seems to believe that we create our own reality totally by ourselves, not that there's some collective stuff going on too. She doesn't have politics about classism. The first time I said something to her about class, she said "Oh, I've worked through all that. I had therapy for years about how my family abused me with money." It didn't seem to occur to her that some of us wish our family had *had* money to abuse us with, rather than having to just do it in the usual ways.

Kelly and I started out team-cooking for our house dinners. But she would come home late, and end up setting the table after I'd been cooking for an hour. When I talked with her about it, she just said she *tried* to get home, but she was so busy with graduate school. Doesn't she think I'm busy, I'm tired after being on my feet all day at the co-op, lifting hundreds of pounds of boxes?

She defended herself by saying she cooked other stuff. I said the rest of us also did other cooking, and this was about us team-cooking for house dinners. When she didn't get home earlier, I finally said I won't pretend this is team cooking and then we alternated weeks. That was an improvement. Except I had to watch after she made dairy dishes even though we had agreed to make our house dinners be wheat and dairy free for my food allergies. Lisa and Judy cooked OK food all the time, but Kelly thought if she did that *most* of the time, that was doing great. Most of the time wasn't good enough when I came home tired and hungry and couldn't eat the group meal.

It's been real hard with her. I've tried to talk to her about it in terms of the class stuff I feel. She says it is all personality—*my* personality. I say I *am* angry when she continues to make classist remarks and assumptions and doesn't listen to me. I'm tired of working so hard when we don't get anywhere. We're at an impasse. An uncomfortable one.

Sometimes I think if I could just get real quick-witted. Like when Kelly gushed over my other two housemates—"all your parents are academics—oh my!" I just sprinkled too much garlic powder and salt on my rice and beans. What if I could have made a toast to all the mill workers and street people!

No one has ever said to me—"Oh, your father dreamed of being an engineer, but had to work in the steel mill to support your family. And then he was laid off and put in a mental hospital. And he died on the street—what an intriguing life!"

Or—"Your mother—she got the nerve to leave your father after he shot her. Then you lived with her parents and she went to school and became a first grade teacher *and* worked at Sears at night *and* made money doing sewing. All that just so you two could move out into a damp one-bedroom basement apartment.

What an amazing woman!"

Sometimes there's no good remark that could cut through it. With the two who are real friends, the classism is a barrier, but I also have good connections with them. It's not fair that I'm spending a lot of energy educating them, but they do listen and learn. It's gratifying when I gain a new ally. Kelly was real surprised that I hadn't eaten seaweed since I work at a food co-op. Lisa knows what I grew up eating and my process around learning about health foods. She joked—"Seaweed didn't come in those turkey pot pies, did it?" It was the perfect thing.

And Judy has been an ally in the problems with Kelly. She also tells about confronting classism she encounters in people.

Sometimes it's still real hard.

Like the time one of them joked about this horrible "wino." They all know my father died on the street. I'm sorry if they had an unpleasant experience with anyone, street person or Harvard frat boy. But I don't hear the same disgust when they talk about nicely dressed men who harass them. That guy on the street was once someone's child, probably someone's lover or husband. He may have a daughter just like me somewhere.

Sometimes it's such a worldview thing. Judy was talking about the wonderful charity things that some Harvard students were doing. They really cared! I talked about how charity keeps people in their places—the superior one who gives help and the one who receives it down below. How I thought what the students were doing wasn't that great—if they wanted to make real changes they could work on their own classism and use their privilege to break down the class system. They could read the work of working class and poor people. They could educate about classist attitudes and behaviors. They could raise and distribute money to grass-roots organizations run by low-income people for themselves. They could work as allies on projects organized by low-income people.

But what I said didn't make sense to them. I guess you have to know what it's like to smile and thank someone for their used clothes even though you hate them. Or get to be the one always on scholarship or financial aid or government benefits. Or go through years of being reminded to be so gratefully nice to a rich couple your grandfather works for who give you an easter basket every year. Even though you're allergic to chocolate and never get to eat even one ear of those years and years of bunnies.

Well, the tea's ready now. Time to go back in. Is this one of those times I'll speak or one of the times when I'll wait for time to pass?

Maybe I'll just go see what they're having for supper downstairs. I bet it won't be seaweed!

Chaia Heller

blondini

"blondini," they'd say in israel
to you and your halo of lemon colored hair.
american raised, i wish i could store up
your yellowness like skeins of yarn,
weave it around my arms

a love for what is lighter than me:
my lust for straight noses,
your great-grandmother's rumpled quilts
thrown so carelessly across your floor
like there are so many more waiting in attics
on both sides of your family

my eye ticking along the ivory face
of your great-grandfather's watch
which measured all those blond generations
and then was tossed down to you so easily

and yet, i shouldn't kvetch.
the diaspora has been good to me
—my skin turns milk white in winter
and my eyes flash cossack blue.
some say i can even pass

but still, i'm not pretty.
look at all i've got to lose:
my great big nose, my great big ass
and my great big anger
that makes me want to call you, "blondini,"
my love, even though i want to look just like you

Nett Hart

Personality or Politics?

We may jump from the accusation, but sometimes some of us women don't much like some other women. Yes, even ardent feminists can find the sisterhood more appealing than the individual sisters. Working together, organizing, socializing, we often fall out over some issue that there seems no way to resolve, there seems no willingness to compromise. We take a hard line. We try to rally opinion to our side.

The incriminating evidence is often anecdotal: she brought tuna to a vegetarian potluck, she used to date your friend, she sat opposite—and I do mean opposite—you on a community board. Sometimes she represents the worst of the oppressors because we can trace back her behavior and *attitude* to some genealogical fault. But whatever incident breaks the magic of community and cooperative effort, we will fall all over ourselves to build our case. Through the betrayal and disillusion we hear hurt, a disappointment of the ideals of community. We want to believe all women are sisters working together to end our mutual oppression. We analyze our disaffection by looking for differences, which serve to create distance between us and give us explanations for why this encounter was sour but the ideal remains succulent. If only we can find a political explanation for why this collective of women doesn't work, we can continue to believe in the possibility, keep giving so much of ourselves to the work, remain open to others in our mutual commitments.

It's convenient—and often true—to pin these irreconcilable differences on politics: she's classist, she's racist, she's ableist, she's so damn cute she must be lookist to ignore me. These political accusations stem from real differences and actual incidents, but we've all had positive experiences of difference with women we respected and for whom we cut some slack. Bad politics seem to surface in those who cross us.

What happens in our feminist organizations when we name politics the reason for dissension is that it polarizes the differences, one caught in her oppressive attitudes and the other caught in her self-righteousness. We find ways to minimize the disappointment by hearing everything from the other as coming from incorrect analysis. Once we determine she's _____ist, everything else follows. It becomes difficult to challenge and be challenged.

Differences do not create strife. When we are working together well it is because all the perceptions and experiences we collectively bring to the project create a deep and satisfying whole. Somebody says and does what you never would, but it is exactly right, a slightly different perspective that nudges our stuck place into the open. And then we're all rolling and feeling good about The Movement.

But other times we get stuck and anchor ourselves to our mutually exclusive positions. Here we create an abyss between us, unbridgeable even if we wanted to. Unreasonable attitudes gravitate to the other as though her bad faith were enough to attract all the forces of oppression. Never mind she has the same scenario circling your pit. This is our opportunity to definitively hang a label on her and her gang that will encumber them through the community.

We need to look again at the intersection of the personal and the political because in repeating that feminist saw we have tended to believe the personal is identical to the political; the political is identical to the personal. In fact it is and always has been an intersection, a particular convergence in experience and understanding.

Our experiences have their origins and are given meaning in a highly politicized world, a world of domination and subordination based on sex, race, age, class, ethnicity, ablebodiness, size, looks, religion, sexuality and education just to name a few. In feminist consciousness we attempt to separate the inherited oppressions and oppressiveness from our sense of self and self-worth so that we relate to one another without perpetuating domination. This process requires a willingness to examine our assumptions and reassign meaning to our experiences so that our sense of being right, being right in the world, and exercising our rights does not stem from entitlement due to dominant/domination status. Concurrently our conscientization repositions our experiences of inferiority, minority and handicap in a political realm.

When there is a clash of feminists it is not because of difference, it is because of a breakdown in dialogue. The large and small differences among us do not create the breakdown but the breakdown creates an opportunity to revert to non-dialogic oppressions, a clinging to the familiar on both sides and a safety within habitual feelings. In other words, our breakdowns, our conflicts, our lies-cheating-and-meanness, happen in a failure of feminist values and a recapitulation to the norms of heteropatriarchal society. In working together it is more important to be women committed to feminist consciousness raising than to be the same.

If, as Audre Lorde says, the master's tools cannot be used to dismantle the master's house, they surely can be used to dismantle the opposition. Our feminist fights, our horizontal hostilities, do not occur because we're feminists or because we're women, but because when pressed to the wall we are willing to use the familiar tools of oppression against one another. As feminists we must disagree, challenge, confront as well as attend, respect, and celebrate one another within a feminist politic. Ending the dialogue is not an option. Going away hurt and angry is not an option. Shrugging it off as personality differences will not do. We are building a movement, you hear? Every time a vital organization dissolves over "personality" or "political" differences, we all lose. Every time a vibrant feminist drops out because it is just too painful to drop in, we all lose. There are always going to be women we can best appreciate at a little distance or to whom at this time we cannot extend the needed latitude. What we need to do is be honest, not blame it on differences in politics or personality but on an unwillingness to enter into feminist dialogue together at this time. This has to be permitted. We can break silences. It is harder to recover from attacks. So whenever one of us gets headstrong and is going to do whatever she is going to do anyhow, let this woman be the one to acknowledge she is acting outside feminism, not from inadequate political analysis or character deficiency, but stubbornness and that occasional need to be stuck.

We have a lot of learned oppression to undo in freeing ourselves from this deeply misogynist and oppressive society into which we were born. Heteropatriarchy is domination based on difference. We need to not make difference a source of fear. In this brave new feminist world dialogue effected by difference creates and recreates the movement. Never rest.

Janet Mason

**A poem for the white middle class lesbian
who insists I am just like her**

Do not attempt
to rub me out
with your generic pink eraser.

Do not assume
I want to pat my lips,
wipe my hands—or my ass—
on your linen napkins.

Do not insist
that our common white
skin and college degrees
make us just the same.

After all,
yours is Ivy League,
enlightening, illuminating;
mine is commuter style,
hard, narrow,
easily put to work.

And please do not tell me
I have risen from the working class,
that I have been graduated,
ordained, anointed,
like a fairy princess,
set free in your perfect
middle class world.

Do not ask me to edit
the fucks, shits, piss poors
and Goddamns from my mouth.

And when you give me
that tight little hostile smile,
don't expect me to repress myself
into oblivion.

When I tell you my story
don't feel sorry for me;
I'm working class, remember—
I can take care of myself.

zana

ability and will

i have rarely been as violent as i was that night.

in the course of a conversation in bed, my lover commented, "but you don't like traveling." i sat bolt upright in bed, grabbed her arms and pinned her down. "WHAT DO YOU MEAN?!!"

for six years i had been *unable* to travel. road fumes made me nauseous. sitting for hours in the same position gave me terrible back pains and joint stiffness. since i couldn't stand or walk much, a long trip couldn't be relieved by "stretching my legs." a car trip of a couple of hours left me too exhausted for any activity once i arrived at my destination. knee problems kept me from driving more than 50 miles by myself, and others rarely seemed interested in going on trips with me and sharing these limitations. i have always *loved* traveling, but haven't done nearly as much as i'd like. for years i didn't have the money; now the obstacle was disability. to be told i did not *want* to travel felt like a slap in the face.

with that lover, as with friends before and since, i have needed to make the distinction between ability and will. what i am able to do, as opposed to what i wish to do.

sometimes that line is blurry. it's true that in a sense i don't *want* to go to a potluck if there will be a circle later that evening; i don't want the back pain that may result from all that sitting, and the feelings of panic and isolation that can go along with being in pain while others enjoy themselves. however i do want the socializing, i do want to eat with my landsisters, i do want not to feel left out once again, i do want the choice of whether to have solitude or togetherness on that particular day, i do want to be able to go to a potluck *and* a circle rather than choose between them.

one currently-able-bodied friend insisted that "can't" wasn't accurate. she said i "could" climb a long flight of stairs—it was just that i chose not to. yes. i was using "can't" as shorthand for "i can't do that without risking further pain and damage to my knee." there are many things i (and others) are technically "able" to do, and we choose not to, and we feel we "can't" because of the probable consequences.

very likely some disabled people prefer to talk in terms of wants. maybe they think of "can't" as stripping away their dignity. sometimes when currently-able-bodied people talk about what i "want" i feel they're politely allowing me my dignity.

but i don't need that. it's a false dignity, a euphemism, a pretense. to insist that we all have the same amount of choice in our lives is a distortion. i live in a trailer with hot running water and a refrigerator and a cookstove and heat while most of my landsisters cook on open fires, bathe outdoors, and live in very simple structures without electricity. i sometimes ask myself if i would want to live as they do, and i don't even know the answer because it is so clearly not an option. i can't even imagine it. when my plumbing didn't work for a week, virtually all my energy went into daily survival tasks: preparing food and washing dishes in tiny amounts of water (hauled by other wimin), finding ways other than a hot bath to ease my aching body, and—most of all—living without a toilet. when it is just so difficult to go and squat outside that i want to cry about it, i've reached my limits of "don't want to" and am into "can't."

as far as dignity, who says it's dependent upon being "able"? mainstream culture, that's who—and i reject that. we all have limits to our abilities, and we all deserve to be treated with respect regardless of where those limits are. i want wimin to respect my dignity by acknowledging the *true* shape of my life. i don't want pity or guilt. and in many cases i don't want help. i simply want my life to be known for what it is. to pretend my limitations don't exist is to say they're unmentionable, unspeakable. *that* is a pity. and though a womon may think she's saying "we're all alike," actually she is distancing herself from me by refusing to relate to the me that really is, the me whose circumstances are very different from her own.

there is language that could be used other than "want" and "can." if some womon asks me, "how would it be for you to go thrift shopping and have lunch?" i can tell her. i can say "i'd love to. i would need you to load my wheelchair into the car, and that we don't stop to do any other errands in town." a woman asked me if i ever go wheelchair dancing. that gave me a chance to tell her how much i used to love dancing, how i miss it, how painful it is to watch others dance, and how i have never felt in safe enough company to wheelchair dance in public.

which gets to another aspect of ability and will. just because a womon's body is capable of doing something doesn't mean *she* as a whole is. it took me a long time to accept this in myself. i felt that because i couldn't (physically) water the garden, put up fences, clean the main house, etc., etc., etc., i *should* do things i'm physically capable of, such as keeping the books and figuring the phone bill. but though i have no trouble putting pencil to paper, my math skills leave a lot to be desired.

another time, a firewood-cutting crew wanted me to have a hot meal ready when they got home. this was an even harder issue, since i'm a good cook. it was difficult to explain or justify my absolute revulsion at this idea—the years of heterosexuality it brought back for me to think of "waiting dinner on the menfolk."

how work is ultimately apportioned on land is a whole other issue; but i want to point out that a physically disabled womon is just as likely to hate a task or be inept at it as any other womon.

"we can carry you" is some wimin's answer to inaccessible land, houses, activities. i'm not real interested in being carried. it means trusting someone else's sure-footedness. it can mean feeling worried, scared and incapable while the carrier enjoys feeling strong and useful. it can bring up anger if it seems that a place could have been made accessible but instead i'm forced once again to be dependent because some wimin decided carrying was a solution. disabled wimin need to be able to decide *ourselves* whether we care to be carried (or otherwise made dependent); just because we *can* be carried doesn't mean we want to. if carrying is really the only possible means of access, i suggest language such as "how would you feel about being carried?" or "we can carry you if you'd like." sometimes we may choose not to go places we can't go under our own power.

when i compare notes with other disabled lesbians, issues of ability and will come up frequently. a few examples:

a womon who is allergic to animals doesn't necessarily hate them. some wimin do dislike animals after years of being barred from the homes of friends with pets. others continue to love animals and feel grieved at having to keep them at a distance.

wimin with environmental illness are not necessarily antisocial. they have severe reactions to chemicals, perfumes, molds, and many other substances. it may be easier to hang out with other environmentally ill dykes, or even be alone a lot, than to go through the tedious task of explaining to each womon all the things in her home and on her clothes and body that they can't tolerate. (by the way, "can't tolerate" is an accurate term when talking about severe allergic-type reactions—not "incense bothers her." it's more than a "bother" when one whiff of something keeps you from breathing freely for a week.) if you care to cultivate a friendship, ask what you can do to make yourself and your space accessible.

food allergy does not equal dislike. on the contrary, people are often allergic to favorite, habitual foods. so don't say, "oh, i forgot, you don't like cheese." it's "can't eat cheese."

a womon with chronic fatigue may well *want* to participate in as many activities as anyone else. rather than assume she isn't interested, friends can talk with her about scheduling, locations, facilities—whatever would make it less tiring for her to participate if she wants to.

a partially sighted womon may enjoy going to movies or creating art. deaf wimin may experience music through its vibrations, and some love to dance. many wimin who use wheelchairs find ways of taking part in rigorous outdoor sports such as canoeing. and some of us do not choose to do these things.

every one of us—disabled and non-disabled—is unique. what our bodies will and won't do, how our spirits operate within those bodies—it's never the same combination in any individual. the best way we can know and respect each other's uniqueness is to be fully there, attentive, leaving behind our preconceived ideas.

Dajenya

does it matter if she's white?

does it matter if she's white?
does it matter
if sistahs and brothahs
look at me askance
not only cause she's a she
but cause she's white?

does it matter
if dykes of color even
think there's something
wrong with me
some auntie Tom
in my soul
some self hate
that must exist
if I would choose
a white woman?

does it matter
if I try to justify
defend
if I point out that
my mother's white
so you see
it's only natural
any relationship I enter into
is necessarily
interracial

does it matter
if I am arguing
because I myself wonder
what's wrong with me
why don't I love a sister?

does it matter
that I secretly keep
a constant eye
for traces of racism
that she thinks she's
devoid of?

does it matter
that she thinks I'm the proof
that there's not a
racist bone in her body?

does it matter
that I don't tell her
how I feel
about her fear of walking through
certain neighborhoods?

does it matter
that I was raped
on Castro Street
at gunpoint
by two white boys
but never in the Fillmore
yet she's afraid
of *my* neighborhood

does it matter that
the "Foxy mama!" whistles of a
young brother on the street
are seen by her as
sexist macho abuse and
her infuriated reaction
is seen by him as
racist rejection, belittlement and
both of them come asking me
(separately)
to take their side against
the oppression of the other?

does it matter that my need
to be accepted as part
of the Black community
influenced my breakup with my white lover
and my subsequent marriage to a Black man
thirteen years ago?

does it matter that
after my divorce
my need to be accepted as a lesbian
threw me headlong back into
a community which in large part
ignores me?

does it matter that
my mother wonders why I contemplate
the color of my future lover
why I ever think it might matter

all these issues twisting my life around
for decades
through my silence

does it matter
that it took me fifteen years
to write this poem?

K. Linda Kivi

Kiss and Keep Fighting

Roxanne's quarters clanged discordantly into the glass fare box. Even her money was angry, Carol thought. Her own change seemed to tinkle mutely and she had to ask the bus driver for a transfer twice.

The two women careened to the back of the bus as it swung out into the thinning late night traffic. The bus was nearly empty but Roxanne sat in an aisle seat. Carol thought about squeezing past her and decided against it; instead she slipped onto the long bench seat that ran up the side of the bus, at a right angle to Roxanne's glare.

No time like the present, eh? "I liked it." If they had to fight over the poetry reading, better it be done with.

Roxanne turned toward her slowly, jaw set, firm but pained. "Didn't bother you it was all white women?" Each word was articulated to a fine sharp point.

Ow. Just let it go Carol. What's your problem? Let it... "Who said it was just about white women?" *Can't leave it be.*

"For one," Roxanne's eyes snared her lover's, "I didn't hear any mention of skin the colour of chocolate, cocoa or ebony." Her sarcasm weighted the air thickly. "Or coffee beans."

The last comment bit hard. Coffee bean was Carol's affectionate, bedroom name for Roxanne. *Why's she mad at me? I didn't set the bloody reading up. Not my fault they didn't invite any women of colour.*

"Well, they didn't say anything about white skin either. Or Japanese. Or East Indian. Or..." Carol knew she'd pushed things too far even before the words finished their gruesome trek from between her lips. Why the fight, she had to wonder? She knew better. She avoided the glare she knew she would find in her lover's eyes. The night lights whipped past, cold neon blue and irate slashes of red, yellow and green. Everything was noise. Nothing seemed to match, or fit together.

Roxanne's face had paled a tone from her even, dark silk brown. She sat quiet and stiff before she decided to answer: "And that pisses me off even more," her voice slipped into the lilt that surfaces when emotions run high, when she talks to her mother, when she murmurs in bed. When she is enraged.

"It's just assumed that all those bodies rolling on mattresses and in sea-beds are white. Or should I say *pink*." She spat pink out with such velocity that a man halfway up the bus turned to look. "If I hear the colour *pink* one more time in an erotic piece, I'm going to puke," she added, glared back at him, pushed her glasses up her nose defiantly.

Bristling silence. Carol tried not to move, not to shift an inch, not to look at Roxanne or anybody else. The bus heaved to a halt. The front doors ripped open to admit a gleeful crowd of six and a few stragglers. The two women studied the newcomers. *Four whitish, one Asian and two black. Wonder if Roxanne's thinking the same thing? She is right, you know. So you got turned on by the poetry. Big deal. The cunt is not a politically motivated beast. Or is it?*

Carol wanted to lash out. She wanted to cry. They had so few evenings to themselves, so few nights in which they could make love with all the volume of their desire, and now this one was shot. Roxanne's daughter Angie rarely stayed anywhere else for the night. It was only coincidence that her school friend was having a sleepover on the night of the poetry reading. *So much for hoping.*

Carol leaned toward Roxanne, who pulled away, as if the distance between them were a force field, something concrete and immutable. Tawny hand took tight brown hand. Roxanne neither resisted nor gave, but she looked at Carol when she spoke.

"Didn't it turn you on at all?"

"No." She was less angry. "Well, yes. At first. But then I just got so pissed off. Not one woman of colour on the panel. Not *one* out of four." The hardness returned to her voice. "It's as if I don't exist."

"You do to me."

"You don't fucking get it, do you?"

"I love you Roxanne." Carol had veered into the realm of the pathetic and she knew it. She wanted, just simply wanted, for the evening to be one of connection and she couldn't seem to let go of the possibility.

"That's not the point. Don't do this Carol. Just don't. Skip it, okay? What is your problem anyway?" she asked but turned away, as if she didn't really want to know. "Let's just go home," she said, her voice flat with weariness. They lived together: one apartment, one bedroom between them, one bed. No couch either. Just piles of cushions surrounded by standing, drooping, hanging and prickling plants. There was always Angie's room.

Angie's room was an island of pastel pink details and cuteness in their household sea of political posters, vibrant colours and unconventional unfurniture. Only the poster of Angela Davis, Angie's namesake, taped to the back of her door interrupted Angie's march into the usual world of seven-year-olds. And Angie was the only element in Roxanne and Carol's life that interrupted their march into the world of total political activity. "Raising a kid is a profoundly political act," Roxanne would remind Carol whenever her presence limited the way in which they could take part in a demo or action. "I don't put her first; I put her beside me, alongside everything I do and believe in."

Politics formed the backbone of their relationship. They met through a South African Solidarity group, ran into each other at rallies, and finally fell into bed together at an Oka encampment. Angie had been in Montreal visiting her father. When Carol was forcibly ejected from her apartment two months later after ignoring the new owner's notice of eviction (after all, they only wanted to add a few shelves, call it renovations and double the rent), Roxanne invited her lover to come live with her. For six months the two women swirled through each other's lives, discussed politics before, during and after sex, inspired each other to more and more, until. Until Carol burnt out, or at least began the slow fade to ashes, an occasional spark still finding flight now and again.

She had tried to talk to Roxanne but couldn't find the words, didn't want to admit that she needed a break, that she needed more of Roxanne's time, attention, whatever. What would Roxanne think? Would she still want her? Carol said nothing and edges grew sharp around their relationship. The argument about the erotic reading wasn't the first. The course of their words was almost as predictable as the route of the bus that lurched homeward.

Roxanne would say: this isn't politics Carol, this is me. My life. I don't ever stop being black. I don't care if it's just a reading of erotic poetry, it hurts me.

And it's all true.

The bus whizzed through the intersection before their stop. Roxanne pulled the cord for the stop bell and stood up, forged toward the door without waiting for Carol. They walked the two blocks home, past the Portuguese pool halls and the empty faces of houses, in silence. The billiard halls were ejecting late stragglers and the world was closing in on itself, all except for the 24-hour bakery where a young, olive-skinned woman washed windows from inside. The Costa Verde was where Roxanne and Carol fetched their Portuguese cornbread and croissants after a long romp in a darkened room or a fast fuck in the morning after Angie had gone to school. There were always buttery flakes between the sheets.

The light in the front hallway burnt out in a sudden blare when Carol flicked the switch. Roxanne tripped over the recycling box.

"Shit, fuck, mutant landlord. If his brain was wired properly, this dump might stand a chance."

They mounted the stairs in the dim shadows of the streetlights, unlocked their door and tumbled inside. Their light worked. Carol, pale and tired, disappeared into the bathroom and Roxanne closed the front door behind her quietly.

The bathroom was comforting. Carol sat on the toilet after she'd finished peeing, enjoying the feel of the cool porcelain ring that circled her bottom. The bathroom had become Carol's favourite room in the house. A refuge. It was the least pitched place in the apartment. Except for the "Which side of the fence are you on?" poster on the back of the door, the walls were filled with cutouts from magazines, images of plants, animals and landscapes some vaguely evocative of women's bodies. It was here that Carol often came to think.

It's true though. There aren't many words for white, particularly not ones with erotic undertones. So many of them are steeped with sexless purity and tight-assed virtue. How depressing. No wonder so much of white women's erotica is about the ocean; it, at least, is blue or tones thereof. Olive is a nice word but I'm not olive by any stretch of the imagination.

Carol's ash blond hair and pallid skin spoke much more of Northern European climes and in the winter, she found herself turning pale and sickly, particularly with Angie and Roxanne for contrast. She felt like a lump of lard, her hips spreading like watery pancake batter in the pan, the flesh on her upper arms flaccid as unkneaded dough. And her back hurt, and hurt and hurt. Roxanne, on the other hand, was leggy and thin and when she complained, which was rare, it was to lament the lack of flesh on her bones. She was often cold, so cold that Carol would send her to run hot water over her hands and feet before she let her into bed. *Thank goodness it's spring.*

Where is she?

Carol abandoned the toilet seat, flushed and turned the light out. In their tiny apartment it wasn't hard to locate anybody. She wasn't in the kitchen or the living room; that left Angie's room—*nope*—and their bedroom. Carol wiggled out of her jeans and pulled off her *Paz y Justicia* t-shirt in the living room. She left them in a pile with her socks and underwear on top. She pried the thesaurus out from a row of tightly compressed books in the wall of bookshelves and studied it for a minute before she headed for the bedroom.

Roxanne was still awake. She sat propped against pillows reading Dionne Brand's latest. *She thinks it's going to win the Governor General's award for poetry.* Carol thought she was dreaming; *since when do they give Governor General's awards to leftist, black, out dykes?* Their African motif duvet, red, brown and black, was tucked under Roxanne's goosefleshed arms. *Coffee bean arms.* Carol sighed quietly, taken suddenly by the vision of her lover who, reading herself into the solidity of colour, had relaxed. There was even the beginning of a smile on her terra-cotta lips. Roxanne's face was wide and round but the angle of her lopsided flattop sharpened her presence. Her body was a similar mix of shapes, her round-round breasts contrasting with the angles of her shoulders, elbows and knees and the whole whetted by her quick movements.

"Alabaster." Carol's thin voice cracked the air between them.

Roxanne looked up, squinted a look of *what?* but said nothing.

"Okay, okay, maybe not alabaster," she looked from one arm to the other, their palest underside exposed to scrutiny. "How about ivory? No... you're right. Not ivory either. That thesaurus is bloody useless."

"What were the other options?" Roxanne was interested.

"Chalk, milk, foam, driven snow, flour, paper and, and... I can't say it... Maggot."

Roxanne whistled. "Come my little maggot into bed with me. How do you like that?" She threw open the covers on Carol's side of the bed. Carol slipped in shyly.

"Roxy, tell me I don't look like a maggot."

"That isn't much worse than soot. I've been called soot black before by some colourblind asshole who thought he was being poetic." Roxanne put her book aside. There was some welcome in the gesture though she still held onto her reserve, tightly, like the duvet. She smiled, slightly, but with a glimmer of opening.

"Those were the comparisons. The adjectives were worse. How'd you like to describe your lover as lactescent, canescent, glaucous, achromatic, leukodermic or frosty?" Carol paused, still hanging onto the thread of her words. "I'm sorry Rox. Hang on, don't say anything for a second." Roxanne's smile slipped back into a straight line of lips. "I've been a shit. It's not you... what I mean is..." Roxanne wasn't giving an inch. "You're right to be pissed off and my inability to deal with it is my problem. I'm so worn out by the isms." *Where to go from here?*

The cat jumped off the dresser where she had been avoiding Roxanne, and pushed her snout into Carol's hand. She felt defeated. Absent-mindedly, she rubbed the cat's ears.

Roxanne was waiting. "Yeah..."

"I had a dream where a bunch of them—the isms—were chasing me; they looked like a cross between a rat and the Tasmanian devil—you know, the one from the cartoons. They were spinning so incredibly fast that I couldn't grab onto any of them. And there were other people there but I didn't know any of them although I had this feeling that I was supposed to." Carol moved closer to Roxanne. "I'm not your enemy. I'm just tired."

"You ever heard the saying that sometimes to be silent is to lie? I can't deal with my lover watching shit go down that affects me and not care enough to say anything, much less give me a hard time for being pissed off."

"It's not that I don't care Roxanne..."

"... Well that's what it adds up to Carol."

Silence again. Roxanne broke it.

"Looks more like sand to me," she said, taking Carol's arm. "Or straw." She ran her dark finger across Carol's collarbone. Carol shivered; the finger was cold.

"And there's food that looks that colour too. You're the chef, what about it?" The finger lifted to Carol's lips, pried them apart, went into her mouth, found her tongue.

Carol sucked in the coolness, swirled her tongue around Roxanne's finger, felt the twinges of the early evening tense in her crotch. Roxanne took the finger out, placed it on the end of Carol's nose, asked: "You know where I'd like to put this?"

Carol tightened her bum muscles and her hips rose faintly under the duvet. For a moment, her face flushed rose and uncertain, desire wrestling with shame. "How about honey?" The change of subject edged around her discomfort.

"Too cliché and too wet. Reminds me of something else, another part of the body." She ran her finger down between Carol's breasts, underneath one, around the other side and back into the fawn crevice.

"I guess maple syrup falls into the same category, eh?"

"Um-hum." The finger was circling, spiraling inward toward Carol's nipple.

"Pancakes."

"Not the way I make them. They look a lot more like me the way I fry them." Roxanne pinched Carol's nipple suddenly. Carol's moan came out, loud and involuntary. "Sorry..." she started to say and remembered. Angie wasn't there. She reached for Roxanne's nipple but Roxanne pulled away.

"No," she teased, "you're going to have to do better than that if you want a turn."

"Brown eggs. Mushrooms. Wicker. File folders. Birch bark." Longing, the growing pounding feeling, almost an ache, was inciting Carol's imagination.

"Oh, I like that one," she laughed. "Can I peel back some of your birch bark sister? How far do you think I'd get with a line like that?" Roxanne reached under the red line of covers and took both of Carol's hands in hers. Carol squirmed down lower, panted as her cheeks touched the cooler sheets deeper in the bed. Roxanne put her lover's hands over her head, on the pillow, and pinned them there with one hand, her long fingers gripping the pale wrists.

"I don't think you're ready to have your birch bark peeled."

"Aaaw Coffee Bean. You're going to need to soon, otherwise we're going to float away in all my wetness." Carol's giggle was cut by the sharp pleasure of Roxanne's teeth on her neck. Sometimes she bit hard enough to leave a mark. Carol arched upward. Roxanne teased. She nibbled on Carol's nipples, one, then the other, blew on them, looked toward Carol's cunt, licked her lips and did not touch for many minutes.

Carol's breath came quicker. "Pine," she gasped.

"And..."

"Shells." Carol wanted.

"No sea images allowed."

Want. "Who made those rules?" Carol's eyes caught hold of Roxanne's and pleaded.

"I did." Roxanne's lips and teeth played with her nipples, her neck, the corners of her lips, her earlobes. One hand still held her wrists. The other feathered her pubic hair.

The cat, curled asleep at the base of the bed, awoke, curious of the movements and moans. She padded up between the two women, through the arch of Roxanne's arm, across Carol's belly.

They both watched as she gave Carol's faintly haired armpit a cursory sniff and swipe of the tongue. She then settled herself in next to Carol's head and began sucking her earlobe, kneading at the pillow where wisps of hair sprawled.

"Not fair. P-p-please touch me, Bean. There's two of you. Stop her. Please." Carol arched up trying to reach her cunt to Roxanne's teasing hand, trying to reach her body onto Roxanne's. She thought she was going to come.

She had to come.

"I still haven't figured out quite what colour you are. Any more suggestions?"

"I," she gasped, "I suggest you stick your finger up my ass." Desire pushed away all but a tinge of shame. Her anus ached to be entered.

Roxanne stopped feathering long enough to reach for the finger cots they kept on their night table. She had to let go of Carol's wrists to put one on. "If you move, I won't. Stay still," she crooned, "stay still." Carol closed her eyes and her centre of consciousness shifted to somewhere below her bellybutton. She was warm—no—burning. She felt exposed. Open. And wanting, wanting wanting.

Roxanne's voice called her back up. "Now, what colour did you say?" She took hold of her wrists again. Slid the latex cotted finger into Carol's mouth to wet it.

Carol sucked hard.

Roxanne took the finger away, like candy from a child. She pinched Carol's nipple again.

"Oh my god, Carol!"

"What? What's wrong?" Panic laid a layer onto her passion before she realized that Roxanne was just, *still* teasing.

"I think this thing I'm touching is..." Roxanne leaned closer, hovering close to the ear that the cat wasn't at. She licked it, whispered, "... it's pink!"

"AAAARGH. Anything but that. Bean, touch me. Touch me already. I want you. Put the goddamn finger inside of me or I'm going to scream. I'll wake the neighbours. I want you. Please take me. Roxy." The last word was a moan.

And then a pause before Carol spoke again.

"Bean, I've got it. I've got it. Croissant. My skin is the colour of Costa Verde croissants."

Roxanne shifted downward, lit the corners of her mouth with a devilish smile. Placed her finger at the opening of Carol's anus. Circled there. Pushed a little.

Carol moaned. Loud. "YES."

"Your turn to go get them."

"YES."

The finger thrust in.

T.C. Robbins

If the Roads Aren't Bad

On her album *I Know You Know*, Meg Christian introduces her song "Ode to A Gym Teacher" by saying the only group of women that may have more impact on young women than gym teachers are camp counselors. From many years of being a camper I can testify to the truth of that statement. I credit some of my counselors with bringing me, whole and relatively sane, out of my teen years. Others, I truly believe, had the goal of pushing me over the edge. Amanda did both.

The summer I was fifteen Amanda became my boss. Still she acted mostly like a counselor. She gave me advice I didn't want, pushed me to do things I thought I couldn't handle and interfered when I did know what I was doing. She also, despite the difference in our ages, listened to me and trusted me. I am told that it was not as much of a risk as I think it was, but still I *was* one of our problem campers. In any case, it paid off. Because she had faith in me, or because I loved her? I don't know.

I do know that I was in love with her. Not desperately (quite cheerfully actually), and not in any sort of adult way, but with an intensity that only a fifteen year old could manage. I don't think I let her out of my sight for the entire three month camping season; it didn't occur to me that this might not be appreciated. That summer I revolved around Amanda in an orbit far more precise than that of most natural satellites. She was who I wanted to be.

Which is not to say she didn't drive me crazy. Amanda is not a hard person to work for, but she is precise and she demands a level of common sense that was just beyond me. When we were in camp I felt like I was constantly underfoot. The highlight of my life was the time we spent out in the van.

Part of Amanda's job was driving the camp van. She got the mail, ran errands and served as the emergency vehicle. Most of the time I was allowed to go with her. I sat in the front passenger seat with my seat belt carefully buckled and felt safe. She never asked me to remember directions or read a map. I watched her sing along with the radio, explain not-for-profit tax-exempt forms to store cashiers and, on at least one occasion, wave french fries at strangers in passing cars. She was the most interesting adult I knew.

And it was in the van that I learned how important I was to Amanda. Being a passenger in a car has always made me sleepy, and no matter how I tried to stay awake, at some point on the return trip I would slump against the seat belt. Amanda not only let me sleep, but she would drive so as not to wake me. Sometimes she would make it over the entire mile of bumpy dirt road that led to our camp, maneuvering around potholes and over rocks.

Later summers I went on to be unit staff and Amanda became the camp director. Our friendship was sometimes strained. As I was given more responsibility and proved able to handle it, I couldn't decide if I wanted to be treated like a kid sister or an equal. And having a crush on someone makes it very difficult to accept that they are not perfect. But I didn't forget those rides in the van.

Towards the end of the summer I was seventeen, I realized I was a lesbian. It was wonderful, it was horrible, it was all the things that falling in love is; mostly it was confusing. My Beloved assured me that being a lesbian was okay by telling me that Amanda was one too. I must have looked absolutely crazy standing outside her door waiting for her to do something lesbian-like, but somehow she figured out what I wanted. We had a long talk about which I remember nothing except that she thought I would probably survive and that it was *not* necessary for me to be quite as melodramatic as I was being.

My coming out didn't change our friendship much. I would call her up and tell her my problems. She would give me advice. I would ignore it. I don't think she ever once said, "Hey, dummy, I know what I am talking about, you are not the first person in the world to either be a lesbian or to fall in love." She certainly had a right to.

I didn't realize how remarkable our friendship was until I went away to college. It was then that I discovered that lesbian communities are often broken up into sub-communities by race, age, and/or politics, and that they don't necessarily mix. At 21 and, more or less, resigned to being myself I can't say I understand Amanda any better than I ever did; to this day when I think of her it is with a combination of chagrin, respect and love. But as Julie Blackwomon says, if we are choosing sides for the revolution, I want her on my side.

Marie Cartier

Come to Me

—for M.

I.
I want to take your secret place
into my cupped hands
and hold you there.
Whisper into your ocean,
"You won. They lost.
Breathe. We are."
Rock a high storm. I want to feel
this sea. I want to feel you
winning this war. Settle
into these hands. And let go.

II.
My face against you, I chant,
"It's over. This place
is different. This place
is different." My fingers shove magic
through your skin. Heal, dammit.
I am lion, grizzly, wolf.
Heal. Let there be light.
Come to me.

III.
You were raped at age ten.
Let there be light. Come to me.
Woman. This small Black Girl you were.
This small White Girl I was,

raped every year of my life—over,
turn over, turn over. I was
twenty-three, and still
turn over. A child prostitute
rarely closes her legs.
Cry for these children.
I beat up mattresses, tear
phone books, smash dishes,
write letters IN ALL CAPS.
And pray. Pray to any goddess
who dares show me her face.
These children we were, Woman.
Black Girl White Girl, let there be light.

IV.
Virginia Woolf said, "I am a woman.
I have no country. My country is
the whole world." I know you do not
feel this way—child of Africa,
beats under your feet,
connection to all there was,
and is, through your hands this soil sifts.
This is not mine to choose.
At this moment, I choose to wrap myself
around woman. You. Woman.

V.
This morning you remembered
a small girl's innocence sprung.
I know those eyes that glaze
become that doll, whose small plastic parts
wheel across the floor.
Breaking. This morning I scramble

for these parts, screaming FIX ME. Screaming
MY MOTHER—my mother
greases my thighs with butter, takes a hot
waffle iron and screams to her daughter,
"THIS IS SEX. DO YOU LIKE IT? IS THIS WHAT
YOU WANT?" I am crawling
on this floor, in my Los Angeles apartment,
thirty years from that kitchen,
sputter no—no no no.
Eight hours from Oakland where you are
remembering, I am yelping—a dog
who wishes to be wolf.

VI.
Bring me wolf. Lion.
Hawk. Snake. Coyote. Bring me to light.
I remember many, many things.
For a long time. I remember.

VII.
And now, you tell me, you remember.
Come to me, then. Come to me.
At this moment, I choose, this country.
Breathe. Come to me.
Let there be light. They will not win.
Wolf. Coyote. Wolf. Lion.
Breathe. Come to me.
Let go. Rock.
Steady.

Sally Bellerose

Martha

Today I was with Martha. Yesterday I was with Martha. Tomorrow I will be with Martha too. Martha is mistress of the slow tease. She's had me on simmer for fifteen years. She lives with her mother Ella. Ella is old and strong and usually home. Martha and I don't get much time to be alone. Sometimes she stays with me at my place, but not for long. I have a cranky roommate and a small apartment with no room for Martha's stuff.

Martha has finally convinced her mother to leave their big comfortable house for three days, to visit her sister. Martha has taken these three days off work. It didn't take much to convince me that this was a good time to visit. Yesterday morning it looked like Ella might never leave. I arrived at 7:00 am sharp. Martha used the direct approach "Goodbye Ma, we want to be alone." But it didn't work. The stuff Martha doesn't take to my house is the stuff that helps her live. Breathing stuff, a metal box with dials and tubes and electrical cords that plug in the wall. Before Ella will leave we had to prove ourselves. We had to prove we could keep Martha alive for three days, alone.

Ella knows that I've come to be seduced by Martha. She doesn't approve. She doesn't disapprove. She watches. She sees my big hands and feet. She sees Martha leaning into me when she walks, hanging on my arm when her cane works just as well. She's seen me pushing my weight in back of the wheelchair every time we stop so Martha's thick graying hair will brush up against my chest. She sees Martha smile. She sees me breathe harder.

Yesterday morning was the first time I had been with Martha all the way through her morning routine. I watched Martha's face and listened for her instruction. Martha watches me as I manipulate her leg into the brace and tug on the heavy brown shoes. Ella watches us. She sees that I remember to check the oxygen tank. She sees that I'm slow.

Slow because I am mesmerized by Martha's delicious slow voice. Slow because Martha tells me what to do in that low rhythmic voice, slowly. Slow because I am inexperienced. Martha does not speak fast and strained like she breathes. She tells me in a measured whisper where my hands go, how hard to push, how far to pull. Sometimes she instructs me with just a look, a raised hand and a half smile.

Ella is not interested in how slow we go. She's worked too hard to help Martha stay alive. She leaves when she sees we can tend to business. When she is gone I am shy. Nervous to be alone with Martha, all the equipment, all this breathing, all this wanting, all this life making itself so obvious. Martha is touched by my shyness. She rubs my head and sings a sad Irish song.

She wants to go out. She wears two scarves, black around her neck and red around her waist. She has bought me a red silk tie and a forties suit. We look damn good. Martha likes it that I can carry the oxygen tank and push the wheelchair at the same time. There is really no need for us to cling the way we do when the Maitre d' stashes the wheelchair at the door.

Martha's hair is piled on her head. It looks even better when it starts to fall. The waiter is impressed with her. He calls her ma'am. Holds the chair for her. Smiles when she orders in French. He calls me "you." When I order Beaujolais with chicken he cuts his eyes at Martha and says, "If that is your wish." Martha likes the way I stare him down. He gets no tip.

We go home and lie on her bed. She takes off her scarves. She takes off my tie. She flops on her belly, says "Rub my back, Honey." I move my hands in big slow circles, carefully. "Like you mean it." I massage harder.

She sits up and takes off her clothes. It takes a long time. She concentrates on what she's doing. She seems far away. I wonder if she remembers I am in the room. Then she slides her hand slowly down her left thigh as her black crepe pants slip to the floor and I am sure she has not forgotten me. She folds her clothes neatly on the bureau. She asks me to hang up my suit. I take it off, throw it on the chair, take off her brace, throw it on top of the suit. She'll scold me tomorrow. Now she asks me to rub her belly, her butt, her thighs. She tells me harder three times. She sings a blues song. The machine that helps her breathe is not turned on, but I am humming deep inside. Martha laughs knowing full well she'll be asleep in five minutes and I'll be wanting her. Knowing that I'll have to wait for morning, when she's ready. But I fool us both and fall asleep first. Martha rubs my head. I dream we're making love. I dream I am completely capable and know exactly what to do, skills Martha will teach me. Such a slow teacher she is.

Colleen Michael Webster

The Measurements

Stretchmarks line my legs
ticking off meals i missed
to fit into your bed

It seemed no matter
how hard i tried
i could never reach
that little space you made
for me to become your lover

Jenni Millbank

Pandora's Egg

How to believe the bizarre circus mirror images that arise after lying with her? To see my own familiar body suddenly writ large by comparison. Writ huge. I am clown, jester, fat lady. I see my flesh drift away in surreal swirls, encompassing larger and larger areas.

Each day I pray for the return of my daily flesh; flesh, always the measure of hot or cold, big or small; the barometre of normality. Now I am tipped off someone else's scales. As I realise this I greet my body as other.

I know, I KNOW I have not changed, yet to be with this woman changes me. She is emaciated and not yet enough for her liking—absorbed by what was popularly coined "slimmers disease." A term so obviously invented by a man who had never starved or purged, whose eyes never ravaged his body with that combination of hatred, anxiety and grief. A clueless euphemism. I am a woman who has a clue, as does my lover, and still here we are, with her tiny and me average, all the world to touch and taste and both of us thinking blandly, repetitively, sickeningly: I'm so fat.

What does it mean, what can she mean to turn to me and say that I am beautiful? How can I ever be lovely to her, as she lies there with her half-of-me body and crazed carve-that-flesh-off eyes? Is she loving me really? Is she desiring me in all truth? Or does she look at me and see saunas, salt-free diets, low-impact aerobic exercise, catabolic food categories? Cellulite. Kilos. Endless clever, narrow, scientific names for what was once a sheer expanse of flesh, loved and lovely. Perhaps I disgust her.

To tell the truth I do not know what she sees when she looks at me. I never ask. I suspect that whatever the answer is, it will be a lie.

When I look at her I see meals half-eaten or furtively thrown up, or both. Lunch for her does not exist, dinner an agony as I wait and watch for the hastily gulped glass of water, the ten minute wait, the trip to the bathroom. When she returns with her eyes streaming, a slight odour still about her, I feel my own stomach begin to churn. Sympathy and disgust battle each other. She is forever saying she has stopped. I bite my tongue. Well, now, truth be told, what do I see when I look at her? Do I love a skeleton, a liar, a woman who loathes herself? I suppose that I do, to be here, accepting her evasions and nursing her through her nightmares. Why is the next question; answering it is altogether too much.

Really, I have too much of a clue to be where I am, which is the humiliating part of it all. I know why I feel this way, and why I should not. Nevertheless, I persist. My body is the slumbering monster, its tameness a disarming illusion, ready to launch forth the moment I lose control. Even lying on my back first thing in the morning, a stomach, which I begin to think of as 'the' rather than 'my,' resembles an egg about to hatch.

For all of this I hate the woman I love. I loathe her for bringing my seeds of loathing into full bloom. Because I know it is in no way her fault, and she has enough guilt and anger in her life, I never speak of it to her. I wonder if she has ever lain awake at night and wondered about me in the way I now wonder about her. I wonder if my resentment creeps out of me in scents and glances to accuse her unawares.

Loving her, from beginning to end, has been a desolation. She has opened Pandora's box for me; wherever I look, I see with open eyes the hatred and hurt of other women, where before I accepted unquestioningly the blasé assurances of "she's just naturally thin/has a small appetite/goes to the toilet after meals/ exercises for fun." I see some of the desperation, hear some of the lies. I imagine there are many more. I wonder where we will ever begin, all these homeless women, not even our own bodies are truly our own.

Funnily enough, after she leaves me, I lose weight. It doesn't make me feel any better. Unforgivably, I have never forgiven her.

Karen X. Tulchinsky

Outside

All the way home from work, I worried. It was the first of November and already the stores were starting their Christmas displays. For me this was the worst time of year. The closer it got to December 25, the crazier the world around me became. Everywhere I looked, people were hanging strings of lights on windows, chopping down baby trees to bring indoors, spending all their money on presents, complaining about it, worrying about whether they should go home for the holidays or not, complaining about that, buying more presents, getting depressed and then pretending to enjoy themselves. It seemed as though everyone in the entire country was losing their minds. This was the time of year when people of Christian backgrounds acted as though theirs was the only game in town. Incredible as it was, they seemed to forget that there were any religions or cultures other than their own. As a Jew, I watched the whole scene from the outside. Every year, it began just a little sooner and lasted a little longer. Each year seemed to outdo the year before, as if it was a contest in extravagance.

All the way home on the bus, I thought about "the holiday season," and how angry it made me. By the time I walked in the door to our apartment, I had worked myself up into a near frenzy. Minutes later, my new lover Marie and I were having our first fight.

"You're so middle class!" Marie shouted at me across the room. "You don't even know how to yell."

"I know how to yell," I lied. "I just choose not to."

"But we're having a fight!" she went on. "You're supposed to yell."

"Why? What good would it do?"

"You'd feel better for one thing. See? You feel lousy right now. I can tell."

"How do you know?"

"You're rubbing your belly." She pointed.

I moved my hand from my stomach. "You don't understand," I mumbled under my breath.

"What?"

I turned to face her. "I grew up with yelling. That's all my father did. Yelled and screamed. I've had enough yelling to last a lifetime. I won't do it with a lover. I won't do it with you." I stomped out of the room and pushed open the door to the kitchen, letting it bang against the wall. I turned on the tap and filled a glass with water. I drank the entire glass and then set it down on the counter. I heard the kitchen door open, but stood where I was, with my back to her. I didn't know what to say next. I knew it would come to this. I knew we would fight about Christmas.

My ex-lover, Janice, never understood, even though we were together for almost three years. With her, the fights were endless.

"How can you hate a Christmas tree?" Janice would ask me. "Look how pretty it is. See? My sister sent some new ornaments."

I remember looking at the tree. It didn't look so great to me. An evergreen tree, chopped down and stuck in a metal stand, dying slowly, covered in coloured balls and tinsel. The first year she brought one home, she didn't even ask me if I minded. I came home from work and there it was in the corner of the living room. I stood in the middle of the carpet, my arms hanging limp at my sides. This tree, this incredibly Christian symbol stared back at me, looming high above. It made me feel like a stranger in my own home, like a traitor to my culture.

That first year I tried to explain to Janice that Christmas was not my holiday. That I had my own holidays, thank you very much, and I'd be happy to teach her all about them.

"What do you mean?" she asked, "Christmas is for every-body. It's not religious any more. It's... North American."

How could I argue with that? She was right in a way. It is North American. All you had to do was switch on any television station, walk into any store, or school, or office and you'd see Christmas, Christmas, Christmas. By mid-December it wouldn't even be safe to go to the corner store any more. By then, every cashier in town would be asking you how your Christmas shopping was going.

"Why shop?" I'd want to say back. "I thought Santa Claus was supposed to take care of all that." Of course I never did. They'd have looked at me like I was crazy.

"Come on, Rebecca," Janice pleaded that first year. "I always do Christmas with my lover. Ever since my mother died, I can't go home for the holidays. It wouldn't be the same. Please baby, it would mean so much to me."

To make Janice happy, I complied. We hung stockings on the wall. We decorated a dead tree. We sent cards to all of our friends. We drank egg nog, sang Christmas songs and ate turkey. I went along, I guess, thinking that it would be a fair exchange between cultures. In December she would teach me about Christmas. In the spring we would celebrate Passover.

In March, one day, I took a bus to the one Jewish bookstore in town and bought a box of Matzah, a book about Passover, and some Kosher red wine. Before Janice got home from work, I spread my goodies out on the table. She came into the apartment and stopped in the kitchen doorway.

"What's that stuff?" she asked, waving her hand towards the table.

"Next week is the first day of Passover. I got this stuff so we could celebrate the holiday. I thought after dinner we could look at the book. It tells the whole story, and there's a part in the back that explains all the rituals and food."

"Oh honey," she said, taking off her coat and opening the fridge, "I'm tired. I had a hard day. How about tomorrow?"

"Okay," I agreed.

But tomorrow never came. Each day I reminded her and each day she put it off, until finally Passover had come and gone. A week later it was Easter. Janice arrived home from work with a huge chocolate bunny for me.

"What's this?" I snarled. I was still angry that she didn't want to learn about Passover.

"What do you mean?" She didn't get it. "It's an Easter bunny, silly. What's it look like?"

"How the hell do I know?" I said icily. "I'm Jewish, remember? Easter is not my holiday."

"Oh god," she groaned. "Here we go again. It's not a religious thing. It's not a matter of Christian or Jewish. It's a fucking chocolate bunny." She threw the rabbit down on the table, cracking it in half, as she stomped out of the room.

"It's not my holiday!" I screamed through the shut door. Then I sat down at the table and began to cry.

After Janice and I broke up, I vowed that my next lover would be Jewish. Unfortunately my hormones don't believe in vows. To my surprise, I fell for Marie, who is French and Catholic. I also vowed that I would never live with a lover again, yet here I was three months into a new relationship, and we had just moved in together.

Standing in the kitchen as I was, I could feel Marie there behind me, but I was too scared to turn around and face her. She moved towards me and put her arms around my waist. Her breasts were pushing into my back. In spite of how mad I was, it felt good with her leaning against me.

"Talk to me," she said.

I didn't know where to start. I was afraid she'd be just as bad as Janice. As bad as all the rest. I couldn't bear it if she was.

"Please," she begged.

"I'm nervous," I finally said, holding my breath.

"Nervous?"

"This always happens to me. It always starts at this time of year."

"What happens, babe?" She lightly kissed the back of my neck.

Oh shit, I thought to myself, might as well get it over with. If we break up, we break up. "It's the Christmas thing," I said boldly.

"Go on..." She continued to hold me tightly.

I felt somehow safe, with her holding me like that from behind. She couldn't see my face. Wouldn't be able to see my fear. I took a deep breath and blurted out, "I hate it."

She laughed quietly. I loosened the grip of her hands around me and turned to face her, puzzled. "What's so funny?"

She smiled at me. "Of course you hate it. I would too if I were you. It's crazy, isn't it? The whole thing. It's so overdone. Like one big, long, loud commercial."

I couldn't believe my ears. She wasn't saying what I thought she would say. I thought she'd defend the holiday, accuse me of being a scrooge, or a heathen, yet here she was agreeing with me. It was too good to be true. "I don't get it," I said, shaking my head.

"Let's sit down, honey. I'll make us some tea. We'll talk."

Later we sat in the living room. I told her about Janice and how she never understood, not after three years of being together. That she never wanted to hear about my life as a Jewish lesbian or learn about my culture. I told her how hard it is being a minority within a minority, especially on the west coast where the Jewish population is small and the place isn't exactly crawling with Jewish dykes. I talked about Chanukah and other holidays and how I missed them, how I wanted to celebrate my own culture with my lover, in my home. How crazy it seemed to me to chop down a tree to stick in your living room, only to throw it out in the trash a week later.

"You know, they don't do it the right way for me either," she said. I didn't understand.

"I'm French. We celebrate Christmas different than the English do. It's not right for me either."

"Then you don't want a Christmas tree?"

"No!" she said to my relief. "What a waste. I couldn't do that. Not at the rate the forests are being chopped down. It would be kind of a contradiction, don't you think? After I just convinced my whole office to use recycled paper."

"Yeah." I laughed. She was smiling. "How come you're so good to me about this? You're so understanding."

She shrugged. "I'm working class. I've been kicked around lots too. I don't know what it's like to be Jewish, but I know what it's like to be left out."

We are so different, I thought to myself, and yet, I feel safe with her. "You're so easy to talk to," I said.

"I want to know about you. I want to know who you really are. It's going to be so important for us to keep talking. You know, we didn't exactly grow up in the same neighbourhood."

"That's for sure." I laughed. She looked so beautiful to me, I wanted to be closer. I took her face in my two hands and brought my lips to hers. She threw her arms around my neck and I pulled her towards me. We kissed with a heat that was more than just physical. It was filled with love and the promise of a future together. In many ways we were like night and day. In other ways we were two of a kind. Outside of the mainstream. Dispossessed. Alone. And Brave.

Yarrow Morgan

On Being Ill

We waited months
for the diagnosis.
After three months
had passed, I grew depressed,
wanting desperately
a clear name, a clear treatment.
The first year I was sick
I was terrified you would leave me,
tire of this woman who sleeps constantly,
is too weak to see a movie,
needs pain pills to sit up
in the evenings to talk.
Happy for the first time in loving,
I couldn't believe it could continue,
nor did anyone else.
The first question every friend,
every doctor, everyone asked
was how it affected us.
I learned quickly
that the chronically ill
are usually left. Meanwhile
we reassured each other
that I'd always been strong,
would beat the odds,
and we could stand anything for a year.

As that year ended
my cat grew thin and weak,
was diagnosed as terminal.

On the day Shadrach died
my dog, Jessie, began gasping for air.
A hole in the wall of her heart
the doctors told me,
managing with massive drugs
to give her six more weeks of life.
Your cat went into grief,
starting to grow ill.
That fall passed in a haze
of sickness, death, and sorrow.
We stopped planning
for when I'm well
except in story-book terms:
we'll take that trip to England,
we'll paddle a wilderness river,
we'll be able to go for walks together.

The second winter we both grieved
off and on for months,
holding each other, naming aloud
the things we cannot have now,
don't know when we'll have again.

Winter is the hardest time.
Bundled in coats, hurrying
to and from the car,
I lose my neighbors for months,
the easy across-the-fence chatting
that when you're gone
is often the only human contact
I have that day. Like Prufrock
I measure out my life in coffee-spoons.
Am I well enough to go to the library?

If I meet a friend tomorrow
will I pay with pain and days in bed?
Can I walk to the corner and back,
around the block, or not at all?
Yet through this time
I've been gifted by your love,
constant as breath,
and come to let in finally
that I'm loved for who I am,
not what I do. You, friends,
neighbors, the animals, my home
all wrap me in love, which slowly
I open to, unable
to do anything now but accept:
the light flowing
through the trees, your touch,
the light flowing through my life.

Robin Wood

Old Women

The first lesbian I ever kissed
       was an old woman.
   I was very young
and thought her beautiful.

She was tall,
     even in the company of six-foot men,
with purple-red lips
       I tried to steal lipstick from.

Caroline was my great-uncle's friend.
    Friend.
Not wife, not lover, but family to him,
         and to me.

Years later, at Easter dinner
    I said I would never get married.
"Good," she said,
    "there's nothing you need a man for."

She smiled at her friend,
         but didn't apologize or explain.
He smiled back.
    I could have kissed them then.

But at 12 I didn't kiss old women
    I knew all the stories—
        ugly, soul-stealing witches,
the natural enemy of little girls.

Caroline died last year, but not before
    I'd come, again, to appreciate
            the strength of those fragile bones.
I leaned over the casket and kissed her goodbye.

Two women danced at her wake,
    eyes wise, heart proud if beating faintly.
        I danced with them.
I should grow so beautiful in time.

Donna Allegra

Navigating by Stars

We never did get to find out just how much of a slut I could be. The message in Whitney Houston's "Love is a Contact Sport" and my dancing to Jan on the refrain "Here I am" conveyed what I couldn't put across with words of my own.

Jan suggested that we go up to the roof to cool off. Hell was cooking at Ronnie's goodbye party in the steaming pot of August. We fabricated conversation on the architecture, the skyline, the dim N.Y.C. stars, glittery like Christmas tree tinsel. Jan brought up the subject of our attraction, startling me.

"Karen, do you want to talk about the tension between us?"

Fear singed my belly. "Tension? Whachumean? I thought we were getting along just fine."

"Maybe I used the wrong word, I guess I mean sexual energy. Are you feeling what I'm feeling?"

My answering thought was, Girl, you just scared the heart out of me. I was all too aware of the juicy ache that stung me ready to sink to my knees. "Oh! Well, I think so" I said, unable to address my desire exposed as a candlelit cake.

It was enough for her to make the first move and we were kissing under the quarter moon. I felt femmed, my back to the wall. Jan seemed so sure of herself. I like these quiet ones, the thoughtful girls who become the group's smart and responsible people.

Her beauty heightened in the moment: her skin luminous, the grey shade of her eyes smoking blue, the flare trumpeting from her nostrils. I could smell her sexual musk, the scent I knew from my own masturbations, a funk I enjoyed on days unwashed in bed.

It took a moment to get the right fit, angling our bodies

together. I caressed her eyes, her neck, her brows, the planes of her cheeks, wanting her to be just as crazy for me. Our tongues danced around each other, exploring our lips and then playing a tug of war, surrendering and taking it back. My fingers traced her face, her hands stroked my back. My heart was pounding through the arteries in my skull, the pulse at my neck, the veins in my arms.

I watched as she touched and petted my hair. That was a good sign—neither afraid nor too curious about my locks. Bravo New Hampshire. Maybe this could be something. I'm a cautious girl. My hopes were high.

It's taken us months to reach this third date, two months of rehearsals during which I felt drawn to Jan while pooh-poohing the possibility of anything to set my stars upon. Still, I'd studied her during the show's run and listened in on her part of conversations when the cast went out for dinner. For weeks I'd been telling my buddy, Randy, that I wanted to jump Jan and hump her on every landing up the five flights to my apartment, but that was jive talking. I'd done some shopping around and what I wanted was for her to be my girlfriend.

****

I can now say that I'm glad the theater world is made up of personalities vying to entertain any audience at hand. That cast for *Dyke Drama* kept me on my toes until opening night. I hadn't been especially enthused when Randy asked me to choreograph for her show, but nothing was happening for me around any dance projects. It was ever a challenge and sometimes a delight to give the cast a nightly stretch to warm them up. They were all non-dancers, but these girls had me hopping.

Dancers pay respectful attention to the choreographer, but this passel of actors wanted to play me like I was a new toy to tinker with to find out how it worked, what would break it, and if it could go back together again. I stumbled a bit before I learned to crack the whip and get those girls back in their places.

All along, I had noticed Jan. She'd frolic in character, but rarely revealed anything about her private self. She did her work within the group, but left off at that.

I wasn't giving her special attentions at first. She just didn't know how to support her back in the stretches and imitated all the worst dancer clichés, like trying for a 180° turn-out. After a while, I knew I was flirting when I gave her corrections. "See how I stick my butt up to bend all the way over? Spread your legs wider for this stretch, now, reach out to me."

After I did my body work with the cast, Randy took over as director. One of her standard rehearsal exercises was to pick a person at random and everyone in the circle gets to ask her any question they like. After Leslie asked me if I had a girlfriend, Diane asked if I liked being single, and Jean if I dated, Jan said, "Would you like to go to the movies, Karen?"

I'd thought, ah, there's the comedienne working the stage, but she followed through. We made a date to see Sandra Bernhardt's *Without You I'm Nothing*. I'd forgotten what a pleasure it could be to have someone's exclusive attention as we talked through Washington Square Park, watching the skateboarders cut sharp corners around the frisbee players and the dirt bike riders zip past mere pedestrians. We sat on a bench by the fountain with a blue-haired juggler in sight. His dropped balls kept rolling our way and I fished some up to his catch.

Jan told me how she'd come from New Hampshire and got involved in Women Take the Stage as a way to connect with other lesbians, then found comic acting was her medium. My trek from the Brooklyn homeland wasn't such a far distance. I told her that jazz dance was the language that spoke best for me, how music in my body was how I could say things.

She walked me home to East 5th Street where I lived next to the 9th precinct station house, and said a lingering good night. I was open for a kiss and felt empty when she suddenly hurried away towards First Avenue.

On our second date, I asked her to Stuyvesant Square Park with its orange and yellow May flowers, after *Dyke Drama* had finished its run. She told me some local gossip—who was seeing whom, who was breaking up, group politics from Women Take the Stage. I could see her listening as I struggled to put words to my excitement about dance class and the performance workshop I'd be doing with one of my teachers in the next month.

She told me, "You were very patient and instructive with us. I went to a jazz class midtown once. After an Olympics warm-up, the teacher said, 'Step, step, jetté, pirouette' and I was like, 'what?' for the whole class. At the end he said, 'Bye everyone. Nice work, and Jan, thanks for the comic relief.' You spoon-fed your steps to us, but what a slave driver! You were so insistent about having the form be precise."

"Well, technique will see you through the long haul every time," I replied, as prim and proper as any deacon.

"I'd like to be around for the long haul," she said. I felt we had just slipped into talking in a different gear and I was alert to her implication. But all she said next was, "I didn't make a faux pas when I said 'slave driver,' did I?"

"No," I said, looking for her to lead.

"I thought for a moment the term might offend you and… well, I'm probably the only white Jefferson around for miles."

"True enough," I chuckled. "There is a historical context to that. Current events too."

We parted as rush hour began crowding down Second Avenue into the East Village. I had jazz class to run to and it took more out of me than a grand jetté pirouette to reach out to her for a goodbye hug. I wanted to invite her to meet me for dinner later, but didn't know how to voice it casually. How is it other women manage to cut the cake?

A week later, Randy called to say Ronnie was moving to California and would I like to come to the goodbye party, and um, could I please, uh, maybe possibly do her the small favor of calling Jan to tell her about it? I thanked her, low key. She said, "You owe me for this, girlfriend. You two will have to name your first child after me." I smiled through the phone and sat quietly all evening.

Jan and I had dinner at Angelica's Natural Foods Restaurant on my suggestion. I felt her gazing at me as I frowned over the menu, unable to decide, as if I ever had anything other than steamed veggies and brown rice. I returned the compliment by spilling my bancha tea onto her knapsack. I had a secret to tell this woman.

We walked down the Bowery to Canal Street, looking for the Chatham Square address. When I took her hand at Houston Street, she held firm. At the door to the party, she stood back and had me enter first.

I could feel the looks pretending not to see when we came in together. I thought, good; it may take a while before what it looks like comes true, but let's get everyone ready.

After we greeted and made our way around the room to connect with people we knew, I couldn't bring myself to say anything to get closer to her, but I could dance. The music was pumping strong and Whitney Houston said a lot for me. Jan struggled to keep up. The boogie clearly wasn't her turf, but I knew she was enjoying my moves. Our eyes connected and held, then I got nervous and broke it off.

****

In the comfort of her arms, the roof seemed a luxurious

domain. "I thought we came up here to cool off," I said to Jan, breaking into the quiet as we held together after a kiss.

"Hmmm. Maybe I made a mistake," Jan teased back.

No darlin, this isn't anybody's mistake, I thought to her, and I made the move that had us kissing again.

Every time the roof door opened, we stiffened a little, but no one we knew had come up so far. Damn: half the fun is being seen.

A little later she pulled away from me slightly, brought my palm to her cheek and rubbed against it like a kitten inviting the caress. "I actually did have a mission in mind when I said we could cool off up here. I wanted to ask for more than another date... What if we take this slow and see what happens?"

"I'd like that."

"When you first came into rehearsal to do the warm-up, I thought, this poor girl will never make it out of here alive. And I wanted to get to know you. You were so polite, almost formal."

"Well, I expected the group of you to be cooperative and interested and even grateful. You damn dykes were terrible children. It was worse than being a 5th grade substitute teacher. Dancers never give a teacher a hard time and hardly ever any back talk. Between Leslie telling me she couldn't do this exercise and Diane that she shouldn't that one because it was out of character and Jean that she wouldn't unless I had sex with her right now in front of everyone, well. And you were no help, making fun of my walk in the improvs."

"It seemed like the only way I could get a piece of you."

"All you had to do was ask," I said, and rubbed my forehead against hers like a kid goat.

The creaky roof door was no longer a distraction to us. No one we knew had come up yet. "Do you have any spare bills so I can get some drugs?" only momentarily broke us apart. I never could keep from cracking up when someone made a good joke. I was treading in a stream of delight, glad to be caught in Jan's embrace.

"So, is this a private party or can anyone have a piece of cake?" Randy demanded. "Well, don't both answer at once, you might trip in the rush to make me feel welcome. Actually, I came to offer a ride home with me and Diane."

I looked to Jan to see what she wanted, found she was checking me out, and she hugged me back to her. "Chauffeur service? Oh excellent good," she answered.

Returning downstairs to the party, my confidence melted to a crumb snatcher's looking to Mommy for cues before hiding a face in her skirt tails. Jan's eyes didn't have much range of motion either, though it felt like everyone else was watching us while looking other ways.

When the car turned into the precinct block, Jan told Randy she'd get out with me and walk to East 3rd Street, her block protected, as it were, by the presence of the Hell's Angels. Sitting together on my stoop, we watched Randy's yellow bug sputter down the street.

"Well, now everybody knows."

Laughing helped. I didn't know my way around this territory. I couldn't even locate myself on the map. I edged near her thighs and widened my legs so as to touch her. Could there be a relationship between us? How did women ask when there was no music to dance to, no props or other people to play out a character with? It was like being set sail at sea and being told to navigate by stars. And riding alongside with that, my disapproving aunts and the scolding sisters from church were frowning on the lapping desire propelling me towards this woman. I was reaching through a haze to catch a falling star with only candles to light my way.

"Would you like to view the N.Y.C. skyline from my 5th floor penthouse?" I ventured. I thought of the phrase Mrs. Baretsky used a lot; it always worked on me. "Karen, please, I want for you to…" I found it hard to refuse my neighbor anything when she approached me with those words. I said to Jan, "I want for you to see where I live and know who I am… and I wonder who you are."

"I'd like to…" her eyes asked more, but her words stopped the question. I had the answer in my pocket. "Well, come on then," and I took her hand, awkward as it was those 5 flights up. Jan followed like a velvet puppy trusting my lead.

On impulse I took us up one more flight to the roof door. "Let's look for constellations," and I handed her the open realm where we'd first touched for holding.

The roof was furnished with lawn chairs where people came up to tan and read during the day. I bypassed these and went to look over the inclined wall whose other face was the front of the building. I turned from the dizzy excitement of looking down from a great height. I was eager as a kid poised over her birthday cake. I stood my back to the wall, one foot planted against it, my thigh turned out, arms spread like Jesus on a cross inviting worship.

The sky was starting to lighten, soon the sun would pour cream into it, but the stars though vague were visible. Coming towards me she asked, "Do you ever wish on the stars, Karen? I'd always wish on more than the first star of the night. One wasn't enough for all the dreams I wanted to come true."

"I could probably decorate the sky with my dreams, given a small portion of the night," I offered, groping.

"I feel like I have two left feet and they're both on backwards."

Jan stood close to me, her eyes still asking more than her words. "You can make a wish for all the lesbians of the world into my breast pocket," I said. I held her head firm to whisper at my heart, now open for all the twinkling stars to listen. I blew out my candles.

Janet Aalfs

What Burns

We walk on a dirt road
through drying cornfields, leaves
curl green to yellow, shiver
in hot wind, damp tassles of silk shine

against blue. My friend wants to turn
around, she says, afraid
someone in a fast car will screech
up behind, stop, leap out

grab her by the hair, drag her
flailing over rocks.
She doesn't have to say who
she means. A sunscorched face

glares from a slowed-down camper
like a sign marked:
"White Only"—words that now
hidden under layers of paint

still smolder, burning everyone.

Mosaic

We float naked in black
inner tubes, my mother

and I on a frog-green
pond, sun-drenched as water

lilies, and my mother's lover
paddling a yellow air mattress,

her hair white spikey
petals soft-blown by breezes,

nothing to hide
ripples of muscle, fat, ridges

of bone and where they meet
in shady dips, deep hollows.

We float surrounded
by a quiet ring

of trees, protected from the road,
skin shining in this rare

haven. The sudden shadow
of a hawk, translucent

mosaic of feathers lit
from above, glides across the dark

pondface, brushing over our bodies
opened as perfect, as brave.

Contributors' Notes

Janet Aalfs: "I know a lot less than I don't know, contrary to what I was led to believe growing up in a white, middle class, nuclear family. A ravenous lesbian, poet, and martial artist (among other things), I exult in learning all that I can about the world."

Donna Allegra is a poet, fiction writer, essayist and cultural journalist. Her work has appeared in *Conditions, Azalea, Sinister Wisdom, Common Lives/Lesbian Lives, The Salsa Soul Gayzette, Heresies* and *Essence Magazine*. She is a performing poet, dancer, and African percussionist. She lives in New York City and works as a construction electrician. She aspires to write trashy lesbian romance.

Paula Amann wrote the love poems herein for C., with whom she shared two rich, stormy years. While they are both Jewish, their different origins in the U.S. and Israel made for distinctive sensibilities, a source of wonder and delight, as well as conflict. Paula owes much to her writing support group, friends, family and the Feminist Writers Guild. Her poems have appeared in *Wyrd Women—Word Women, New Poetry,* and *Rambunctious Review*.

Sally Bellerose is a writer and nurse living in western Massachusetts. Her work has appeared in numerous publications including *Sojourner, Word of Mouth, Caprice,* and *Hurricane Alice*. Her work is scheduled to appear in several anthologies, including *Women's Glibber, For Appearance Sake,* and *The Poetry of Sex: Lesbians Write the Erotic*. She is working on her first novel.

Gwendolyn Bikis: "I live in Oakland, California, where I do literacy work alongside my writing. I am a member of the Oakland Black Writers' Guild, and an MFA student in Creative Writing and Literature at Goddard College. Excerpts from my as-yet-uncompleted novel have been published in *Conditions, Common Lives/Lesbian Lives,* and *Catalyst*. Another excerpt is forthcoming in *The Persistent Desire*, edited by Joan Nestle. I have a sun in Capricorn, a moon in Virgo, and a rising sign in Scorpio. The ocean is my favorite place."

Marie Cartier has published in *Pudding, Focus, Eidos, Kalliope, Eve's Legacy, Central Park, Earth's Daughters, Sinister Wisdom,* and *Heresies,* among others. Currently, she is the Artist in Residence at the Alcoholism Center for Women in LA, in the first residency the California Arts Council has ever funded specifically for incest survivors.

Elizabeth Clare: "I am a lesbian/feminist activist, poet, and essayist, transplanted from the Pacific Northwest to the Midwest. I am currently getting my M.F.A. in Creative Writing at Goddard College."

Diana Aleyn Cohen is a 26-yr-old lesbian of East-European Jewish and West-European WASP descent. Her poems have appeared in several journals, and her book-length manuscript, *The Regeneration of Wings,* is currently seeking a publisher. She works in Portland, OR, as an apprentice carpenter. The lover about whom she wrote "Cancer Poem" continues to live with both Ewing's sarcoma and cardiomyopathy sixteen years after her initial cancer diagnosis.

Dajenya is an African-American/Jewish poet/writer. She lives in the San Francisco East Bay with her two wonderful sons. She is studying clinical psychology in preparation for a career working with children and/or families in need. Her life is very fulfilling, but Dajenya still dreams of having a lover some day (of *any* color!).

Debby Earthdaughter: "I'm 30, from German/unknown heritage. I'm now living alone and working on a land trust for women with disabilities (I'm chemically sensitive now). I've learned to like sea veggies and actually ordered a whole *pound* of nori with my lover. I plan to introduce it into generic macaroni and cheese so all those potential dykes from my old neighborhood won't have such culture shock later in life."

Amy Edgington is a disabled Lesbian writer and artist, living in the South. Her poetry also appears in *Sinister Wisdom* and *Heresies*, and in *Wanting Women: An Anthology of Erotic Lesbian Poetry* and other anthologies.

Berta Freistadt: Lives in London—writes prose and poetry. Has been published by: Sheba Feminist Press, The Women's Press, Chatto & Windus, The Oscars Press, Crossing Press, Hutchinson, Onlywomen Press & Virago.

Jan Hardy: Editor of *Wanting Women: An Anthology of Erotic Lesbian Poetry* and author of *out here flying*. Her poetry and prose have been published in various lesbian/feminist journals and anthologies. She is a new member of the Gertrude Stein Memorial Bookshop collective in Pittsburgh, and she loves to publish and promote lesbian writing.

Nett Hart is a wild Lesbian living in the country where she writes, builds, tinkers, gardens, does alchemy, clay and laundry. She is a founding member of Word Weavers, a Lesbian publisher and of Creating A Lesbian Future, a producer of multicultural Lesbian events. She is a graphic designer, administrator for Lesbian Natural Resources, and the author of the book *Spirited Lesbians: Lesbian Desire as Social Action*.

Chaia Heller was born in Stamford, CT and has spent the last ten years living in Iowa and Vermont where she has taught women's studies at Burlington College and the Institute for Social Ecology. She has been a psychotherapist, activist, speaker and poet for years, dealing mainly with issues of women's creativity and liberation. She is a member of the "Speak Out" speakers bureau, sponsored by South End Press, and she tours nationally, speaking on issues of feminism and ecology. Her poetry has appeared in such periodicals as *The Grinnell Review, Sinister Wisdom,* and *The Burlington Review.* She currently lives in Western Massachusetts where she teaches, gives workshops and writes.

April Jackson is a 20 year old student living and fighting in Greensburg, PA. Amy is her life partner as of April 5, 1990. April is working towards a bachelor's in communication/women's studies and embarking on a documentary. "The only reasons to keep on fighting are love, philosophy and the education of women about women."

Jodi: "Disabled Jewish Dyke. Editor of *Hikane: The Capable Womon*, disabled wimmin's magazine. Have experienced ageism (the two-headed discrimination... in my case received on the young end of the scale), ableism, and anti-Semitism first-hand. Am also committed to supporting fat politics and opposing racism. Been on both ends of class warfare."

Joanna Kadi is a working-class, able-bodied, Arab-Canadian lesbian feminist. She is a political activist and writer who is currently editing an anthology of writings by Arab-Canadian and Arab-American feminists (to be published by Kitchen Table: Women of Color Press).

K. Linda Kivi: "I am an Estonian-Canadian dyke who lives in the mountains of interior British Columbia. This story is a salute to women's anger (though it often scares the shit out of me). Sigh: we've got *so* far to go still."

Sandra Lambert: "I originally wrote this essay in 1987. Since then, due to post-polio syndrome, I've quit my job, live on disability, and use a wheelchair full time. I am no longer considered a 'worker' in this society. I am happier than I ever have been. This essay is dedicated, as always, to Eleanor Smith for our thirteen years of talking disability, and also to Beckie, who continues to be my friend in the largest sense of that word."

Janet Mason's poetry and fiction have appeared in numerous anthologies and journals including *Wanting Women*, from Sidewalk Revolution Press, *Word of Mouth*, from Crossing Press; *Sojourner, Common Lives/Lesbian Lives, Matrix,* and *Fireweed*.

Jenni Millbank: "I'm a feminist, live in inner city Sydney, work in law reform, plan to write the definitive annotated bibliography of lesbian cinema (way too much of which will say, 'don't see this, it's terrible'), love gelato, read a lot, and generally find it very hard to sum myself up in 50 words or less."

Pam Mitchell is a working-class writer, activist and clerical worker who has been on the staffs of numerous publications, including *Sojourner, Gay Community News* and *Second Wave.* She writes fiction as well as non-fiction, and has written most extensively about issues of class, race, and Jewish identity, and about the politics and effects of child sexual abuse and sexual exploitation by health care providers.

Yarrow Morgan: "I am a 44 year old white, working-class lesbian who has been disabled for the past 2-1/2 years with Chronic Fatigue Syndrome. I've had poems published in several magazines, & in the anthology *I Never Told Anyone.* I co-edited *Voices in the Night,* & am the author of *A Winter House.*"

Bonnie Morris: "I am a Jewish lesbian writer and a professor of women's studies, able to leap tall histories at a single bound; I present a one-woman play about Jewish women's identity at music festivals and feminist conferences; I collect stories, take photographs, watch, listen, love women; you've seen me around."

T.C. Robbins: "I seem to only write when I am supposed to be working on graduating from some school or another. Writing is how I cope with a world that I want to make more sense than it does. My first publication was in *Lesbian Bedtime Stories.*"

Sue Russell is a graduate of the University of Pittsburgh's Writing Program whose poetry has appeared in such publications as *5 a.m., Pennsylvania Review, Folio, Black Swan Review,* and *Laurel Review.* In the lesbian community, she has served as marketing director for Pittsburgh Women's Cultural Corporation (a.k.a. Bloomer's Restaurant).

Cristina Salat: "*Living in Secret,* my first novel, will be out from Bantam January '93. My fiction and non-fiction appears in *Popu-*

lar Photography, Delta Scene, Pub, Whiskey Island Magazine, Sacred River, Dyke Review, Writing For Our Lives Literary Journal, and *Planet Roc.* Basically I'm a full-time writer, generally trying to prove that the impossible is possible."

Susan Stinson's poetry and fiction have appeared in many magazines and anthologies, including *The Kenyon Review, Sinister Wisdom, Yellow Silk* and *Word of Mouth,* volumes 1 and 2 from The Crossing Press. She gives fat liberation workshops, and has completed a novel, *Fat Girl Dances With Rocks.*

Ruth L. Schwartz: "Although I've written all my life, it was after coming out as a lesbian (in 1982) that I turned to poetry more seriously. I've published poems in numerous journals, and in 1991 won first place in both the Nimrod/Pablo Neruda and New Letters awards. The S.F. Bay Area is my chosen home."

Karen X. Tulchinsky: "I am a middle class, Jewish lesbian who was born and raised in a big city in Eastern Canada. My lover is a working class, French, ex-Roman Catholic lesbian who was born and raised in small villages in the Prairie Provinces. In spite of our differences, (or maybe because of them) we fell madly in love 'on sight,' and have been together ever since (almost eight years). My work will be appearing in two other anthologies, one published by The Women's Press in Toronto and one by The Crossing Press in Santa Cruz, California."

Lois Van Houten: "I'm 73, born in 1918, Scorpio, am a married woman who did not realize what I really was until age 52. Stayed with the marriage for all sorts of reasons. Have a son 40, another 48... yearn, sometimes, for a true woman companion."

Colleen Michael Webster is currently writing her dissertation on Muriel Rukeyser, reclaiming her for a larger audience. Living on the Gunpowder River in a Baltimore suburb with her three faithful cats, Colleen runs, sails, bikes, windsurfs, rollerblades and anything else to keep her outside.

Robin Wood is a 21 year old Black Lesbian who comes from a long line of strong, proud women. She has recently signed a 13 month lease with her lover of nearly 3 years, ending the stage of their relationship where they lived in different states. She has stories forthcoming in *Common Lives/Lesbian Lives*.

zana: "disabled jew, 45, approximately lower middle class. i'm very excited to be working with SHE land trust toward more lesbian communities, and toward those communities including more different kinds of dykes. living with diversity is very challenging, but we can grow from it, too..."

Suggestions for Further Reading

Books

Compañeras: Latina Lesbians (An Anthology), compiled and edited by Juanita Ramos (N.Y., NY: Latina Lesbian History Project, 1987)

Cultural Etiquette: A Guide for the Well-Intentioned, by Amoja Three Rivers (distributed by Market Wimmin, Box 28, Indian Valley, VA 24105), 1990

A Gathering of Spirit: A Collection of North American Indian Women, edited by Beth Brant (Degonwadonti) (Ithaca, NY: Firebrand Books, 1988)

Home Girls: A Black Feminist Anthology, edited by Barbara Smith (Latham, NY: Kitchen Table: Women of Color Press, 1983)

Long Time Passing: Lives of Older Lesbians, edited by Marcy Adelman (Boston, MA: Alyson Publications, Inc., 1986)

Look Me in the Eye: Old Women, Aging, and Ageism (expanded ed.), by Barbara Macdonald with Cynthia Rich (San Francisco, CA: Spinsters Book Co., 1992)

Making Face, Making Soul: Haciendo Caras: Creative and Critical Perspectives by Women of Color, edited by Gloria Anzaldúa (San Francisco, CA: Aunt Lute Foundation Books, 1990)

Nice Jewish Girls: A Lesbian Anthology (rev. & updated ed.), edited by Evelyn Torton Beck (Boston, MA: Beacon Press, 1989)

Over the Hill: Reflections on Ageism Between Women, by Baba Copper (Freedom, CA: Crossing Press, 1988)

Piece of My Heart: A Lesbian of Colour Anthology, edited by Makeda Silvera (Toronto, Ontario: Sister Vision, 1991)

Shadow on a Tightrope: Writings by Women on Fat Oppression, edited by Lisa Schoenfielder and Barb Wieser (San Francisco, CA: Aunt Lute Foundation Books, 1983)

This Bridge Called My Back: Writings by Radical Women of Color, edited by Cherríe Moraga and Gloria Anzaldúa (Latham, NY:

Kitchen Table: Women of Color Press, 1984)

Tribe of Dina: A Jewish Women's Anthology, edited by Melanie Kaye/Kantrowitz and Irena Klepfisz (Boston, MA: Beacon Press, 1989)

With the Power of Each Breath: A Disabled Women's Anthology, edited by Susan E. Browne, Debra Connors, and Nanci Stern (Pittsburgh, PA & San Francisco, CA: Cleis Press, 1985)

Yours In Struggle: Three Feminist Perspectives on Anti-Semitism and Racism, by Elly Bulkin, Minnie Bruce Pratt, and Barbara Smith (Ithaca, NY: Firebrand Books, 1984)

Journals

Bridges: A Journal for Jewish Feminists and Our Friends (P.O. Box 18437, Seattle, WA 98118)

Broomstick: A Quarterly National Magazine By, For, & About Women Over Forty (3543 18th St., #3, San Francisco, CA 94110)

Dykes, Disability, and Stuff (DD&S, P.O. Box 8773, Madison, WI 53714), available in standard print, large print, or braille

Fireweed: A Feminist Quarterly (P.O. Box 279, Station B, Toronto, Canada M5T 2W2), Issue #16, "The Issue Is 'Ism: Women of Color Speak Out," Issue #25, "The Issue Is Class," Issue #26, "Is Class, Too," and Issue #35, "Jewish Women"

Hikane, The Capable Womon: Disabled Wimmin's Magazine For Lesbians & Our Wimmin Friends (P.O. Box 841, Great Barrington, MA 01230), available in print, braille or tape

Lesbian Ethics (L.E. Publications, P.O. Box 4723, Albuquerque, NM 87196), Spring 1991 issue on class

Sinister Wisdom (P.O. Box 3252, Berkeley, CA 94703), Issue #39, "On Disability," Issue #45, "Lesbians and Class" and Issue #47, "Tellin' It Like It Tis" edited by a collective of Lesbians of Color

Also available from Sidewalk Revolution Press:

Wanting Women: an Anthology of Erotic Lesbian Poetry
edited by Jan Hardy

"The poets in this collection shout, sing, whisper and croon their words of tenderness, anticipation, lust and love. Engaging all of our senses, these poets present lesbian sexuality with liveliness and zest."
—Robin Becker, poetry editor of *Women's Review of Books*

Includes Marilyn Hacker, Jacqueline Lapidus, Leslea Newman, Tee Corinne, Joan Nestle, and many more.

Individual orders $9.95 plus $1.50 postage and handling, pre-paid, to Sidewalk Revolution Press, P.O. Box 9062, Pittsburgh, PA 15224. Bookstores may order from Inland Book Co., Bookpeople, or Bookslinger.

Wanting Women $9.95
ISBN: 0-96174096-1-2